Separate Pasts

Growing Up White in the Segregated South

Separate Pasts

Melton A. McLaurin

Brown Thrasher Books
The University of Georgia Press
Athens and London

Growing Up White
in the Segregated South

Second Edition
With a New Afterword by the Author

© 1987, 1998 by the University of Georgia Press
Athens, Georgia 30602
www.ugapress.org
All rights reserved
Designed by Sandra Strother Hudson
Set in 10 on 13 Century Old Style

Most University of Georgia Press titles are
available from popular e-book vendors.

Printed digitally

Library of Congress Cataloging-in-Publication Data

McLaurin, Melton Alonza
Separate pasts: growing up white
in the segregated South / with a new afterword
by the author, Melton A. McLaurin.—2nd ed.
176 p. : ill., map; 22 cm.
ISBN 0-8203-2047-1 (pbk. : alk. paper)
"Brown thrasher books."
1. McLaurin, Melton Alonza—Childhood and youth.
2. North Carolina—Race relations.
3. Wade (N.C.)—Race relations. I. Title.
E185.93.N6 M35 1998
305.8'009756—dc21 98-015522

ISBN-13: 978-0-8203-2047-2

British Library Cataloging-in-Publication Data available

On the title page: The author's grandfather
standing in front of his first store, circa 1951.

To Megan, with hope

Contents

Acknowledgments

I discovered soon after beginning this book that writing from experience is not an easy task. Trained as a historian, I longed for the sense of security that the research data contained in my file cards had always provided. I also missed the protection that research notes furnished, allowing me to write with relative objectivity, as the observer removed in both time and space. I now found myself drawing upon memory, the most subjective of all sources. All my recollections of the past, both painful and pleasant, were, I realized, an inseparable part of my most fundamental concepts of self.

Under these circumstances, I found my colleagues' comments about the manuscript invaluable. Mavis Bryant, formerly of the University of Tennessee Press, graciously agreed to read an early draft. Her thorough and perceptive review was much appreciated. Without it, the work would never have been completed. Barbara Klein, my sister-in-law, helped persuade me that others might find my personal experiences with and responses to segregation interesting and enlightening. The critiques of colleagues at the University of North Carolina at Wilmington, especially those of John Haley and Carole Fink of the Department of History and Sylvia Polgar of the Department of Sociology, were extremely helpful. Finally, the suggestions, comments, and encouragement of Dr. Hubert Eaton, who devoted much of his life to transforming the segregated South, helped persuade me that memory, although subjective, remains a valuable source of both fact and truth, even for the historian.

Separate Pasts

Growing Up White in the Segregated South

The author as a high school student working in his grandfather's store

Prologue

The bright orange bus rolled slowly to a halt, warning lights blinking, stop sign extended. A constant babble of exuberant young voices poured from the bus's open windows. White faces and arms poked out from the windows, the arms waving, the heads turning to shout at the children who played in the schoolyard across the highway. I stepped down from the bus to the shoulder of the road and then walked in front of the bus across the gray concrete. I heard the bus drive off, noticed the high whine of the engine before the driver shifted to second gear. I walked up the graveled drive, between the gasoline pumps that stood on their whitewashed island, beneath the big red, white, and blue ESSO sign. I paused for a moment before opening the screen doors of the store.

The kids from the school next door swarmed about me now. They were sweaty from playing in the hot sun of the early afternoon, and they screamed and yelled at one another, ignoring me as they darted about as if propelled by sudden bursts of energy. For the most part their dress differed little from my own or that of the friends I had left on the bus. The boys wore high-topped tennis shoes, blue jeans, and short-sleeved cotton shirts of a variety of colors. The girls wore either knee-length pastel cotton dresses or starched white cotton blouses, wilted by the heat, over full dark skirts hemmed at the knees. Below both skirts and dresses were the inevitable oxfords, topped by turned-down white bobby sox. All these colors flashed by me, like the fragments in a gigantic kaleidoscope. Yet one color had more significance than the others.

The open, laughing faces and the frantically active limbs of the children who ran back and forth from store to schoolyard were black. They lived outside my world and the world of the white children on the bus that had transported me from my seventh-grade classroom to my grandfather's store on that September day in 1953. I stood for a moment watching them play and then walked through the door into the store, and into their lives.

The Village

Wade was much more than the village in which I grew up. For eighteen years it was, practically speaking, my entire world. As a youth I believed Wade to be representative of the world that lay beyond my limited experience. It was, I thought, typically American. Occasionally a radio or television program or a newspaper headline would hint that perhaps Wade differed from much of the rest of the country. It never occurred to me, however, that rather than being representative of the nation as a whole, Wade was in fact an almost perfect microcosm of the rural and small-town segregated South. The social patterns of the village had emerged after Reconstruction, had been refined by the turn of the century, and had not changed much since. The Wade of 1953, I later learned, differed little from that of 1933, or for that matter, except for the presence of automobiles and electricity, from the Wade of 1893.

Wade's white residents, all of whom I knew personally and most of whom I saw at least once a week, were decent people—honest, law-abiding, God-fearing. Steeped in traditional values, they, like most white southerners of the era, were convinced that the South had always been, and would remain, a white man's country. With few exceptions, the white people of Wade were satisfied with their community and relatively unconcerned by events in the outside world, or so it seemed to me at the time. Of course, I had few means of comparing life in Wade to that in Georgia or Virginia, and even fewer of comprehending the realities of life in places so foreign as New York and California.

The past, on the other hand, was a palpable reality in the Wade of my youth. For all of my life I had been nurtured on tales of the past, stories of family events and local occurrences that I had come to know by heart. I was also well versed in racist dogma, having been instructed from birth in the ideology and etiquette of segregation. Caught up in the rhythms of village life, I naturally assumed that the stable, constant Wade with which I was so familiar, the ordered village life my father, grandfather, and great-grandfather had known, would go on forever. It was unimaginable that mine would be the last generation to come of age in the segregated South, and that the Wade I knew would soon collapse beneath the irresistible pressures brought to bear upon it by the forces of social change.

In retrospect, the warnings that change was afoot seem obvious. I grew up in Wade during the 1940s and 1950s, when rumblings of racial change were in the air but before the tumultuous civil rights struggles of the 1960s. It was no accident that the people of Wade seemed so oblivious to the forces of change that were so clearly discernible to people outside the South. In fact, they chose to ignore all signs of change, as if by a conscious act of will they could suspend the course of history and retain the customs of a cherished past. The reaction of Wade's whites to the Supreme Court's historic decision in the 1954 Brown school desegregation case, for example, was typical of their response to attacks upon segregation. The ruling concerned them, but they remained convinced that the South would find an acceptable method of circumventing it. Such convictions were constantly reinforced by the pronouncements of leading public figures of the state and region.

Because I knew them so intimately, the people of Wade struck me as unique. In reality, however, they were no different from the inhabitants of hundreds of other small towns and villages that dotted the rural landscape of the South. The village was located in the heart of the cotton and tobacco country of southeastern North Carolina, and its residents were no more than a generation or two removed from the farm. Though merchants, tradesmen, and professional people now, they loved the land and retained their ties to it. Most tended a family garden and kept a few chickens, as did my family. Some raised a pig or two each year; others kept a cow to ensure fresh milk and butter for the table. Not only were the village residents physically tied to the land; they thought as rural people do, adopting new ideas and institutions slowly, clinging to the reassuring stability of family, church, and community. For the most part, Wade's residents were no more affluent than the families who remained on the farms that ringed the village and with whom they shared social, economic, and kinship bonds. The outlying farms sustained village economic life, just as farmers continued to determine Wade's social and cultural patterns.

Wade had begun some time in the second half of the eighteenth century as a boat landing on the Cape Fear River, but river traffic had long ceased by the time of my childhood. The village I knew had grown up about two more modern transportation arteries, which carried produce from and supplies to the surrounding farmlands. The Atlantic Coast Line Railroad, which had arrived late in the nineteenth century, sliced through the heart of the village. Until the late 1950s it played a vital role in the local economy. Farmers shipped cotton, watermelons, and other crops from the railway depot, an elongated frame building with wooden loading docks, which received trainloads of fertilizers and agricultural implements from factories and warehouses in coastal cities. Throughout most of my boyhood, steam-driven engines puffed and wheezed to a stop to pick up or discharge passengers. Local postal service depended upon the passenger trains, and waiting for Number 89 to deliver the morning mail was a favorite pastime for the boys of the community. So, too, was climbing over and into the empty boxcars that were shunted onto the rail spur that ran northward past the depot up to the gin and sawmill.

United States Highway 301 ran through the town's east side and connected Wade with the larger towns of Dunn, thirteen miles to the north, and Fayetteville, twelve miles to the south. Both towns possessed the services and amenities that Wade so obviously lacked—department stores, hospitals, theaters, restaurants, and

the tobacco markets where the region's most important cash crop
was sold. The highway also brought Yankee tourists through on
their way from New York or New England to Florida. Occasionally
the tourists stopped at one of the six combination grocery store–
service stations that lined the highway's often-resurfaced lanes.
There the cramped, road-weary passengers stretched their legs
and purchased soft drinks and snacks while their cars were being
filled with gasoline. The tourist trade brought welcome dollars to
the village economy and confirmed the locals' conviction that north-
erners talked funny.

The sawmill and cotton gin, both of which were located west of
and adjacent to the railroad, employed a number of Wade's residents, black and white. The gin provided only seasonal work, for it
stood idle except in the fall during the cotton harvest, when it
cleaned the crop brought from local fields. While most farmers
trucked in their raw cotton, it was not unusual to see wagons filled
with cotton pulled by a team of mules. The sawmill, which ran full
time, employed a large percentage of Wade's men. Its huge, unguarded blades sliced through lumber from trees felled by loggers
in nearby pine forests. Behind the mill, piles of rough lumber in all
lengths and widths covered acre upon acre, providing an inviting,
and dangerous, playground for the older village boys.

Both mill and gin belonged to Clarence Lee Tart, a bear of a man
with icy blue eyes and bushy white eyebrows. His family had made
a small fortune in the lumber business and owned a considerable
amount of real estate in Wade. Mr. Tart was rumored to be worth
the magical sum of one million dollars. I stood in awe of the man,
who, seated behind a paper-littered desk, represented the ultimate
in wealth and social position. He was the only man I ever heard my
father and grandfather speak of in a deferential manner, and I
sensed from their remarks the power the man held over much of
the village economy. In fact, no resident had a greater impact upon
life in Wade than he did, and although he maintained a small office in
Wade, he chose to live in Dunn, away from the mill workers and
loggers upon whose labors his fortune rested.

The village had been incorporated once, with a regular police force and city officials, and, of course, taxes. The luxury of incorporation was abandoned with the Depression. People, my grandmother often explained to me, simply couldn't afford city taxes, and so Wade reverted to its former status of unincorporated hamlet. The old corporate boundaries, however, somehow survived. Officially, Wade was one mile square. Most of its homes and businesses clustered in a considerably smaller area, a rectangle roughly the size of a city block. The village center was bordered on the north and south by streets that ran approximately half a mile from the highway to the railroad. The highway formed its eastern border, and on the western edge a short street paralleled the railroad, connecting the northern and southern boundary streets. Beyond this central block a network of one-lane dirt roads wound into three outlying residential areas, all populated by blacks. The street that formed the southern boundary of the block continued westward across the railroad into a small white residential neighborhood. Along the highway to the north of the village center was located yet another large black community, while the homes of whites lined the highway south of the village.

Wade was not a pretty village, nor was it ugly. It was simply plain. Until the early 1950s its streets, except for the highway, were unpaved and traveled frequently by mule and wagon as well as by automobile. In the summer and fall clouds of dust stirred by the village traffic coated Wade's houses and people. Fortunately, frequent afternoon thunderstorms drenched the town, their downpours leaving the village once again clean, if not sparkling. The rains created dingy brown puddles where the streets curved, eyesores to the adults and an irresistible invitation to the children. Pushing toy boats fashioned from scrap boards pirated from Mr. Tart's lumber yards, we waded happily into the puddles despite the grownups' warnings that we would catch ringworm and other assorted ailments.

The village houses did little to enhance Wade's appearance. In the entire community there was but one brick home and fewer than

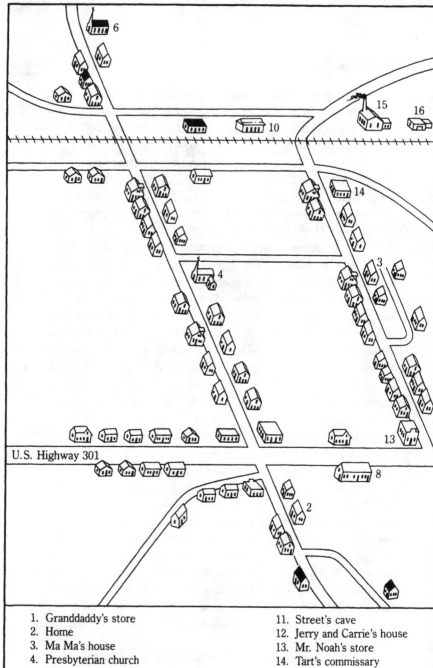

6

15   16

10

14

3

4

13

8

U.S. Highway 301

2

1. Granddaddy's store
2. Home
3. Ma Ma's house
4. Presbyterian church
5. Baptist church
6. African Methodist Episcopal (AME) church
7. AME Zion church
8. White elementary school
9. Black elementary school
10. Depot

11. Street's cave
12. Jerry and Carrie's house
13. Mr. Noah's store
14. Tart's commissary
15. Sawmill
16. Cotton gin
17. Betty Jo's house
18. Viny Love's house
19. Dora Lou's house

Atlantic Coast Line RR

11

The Bottom

19

7

17

5

1

9

12

18

White residence or business

Black residence or business

The Village

a dozen "nice" frame houses. Most of the larger homes possessed neither grace nor elegance. Though solid and comfortable for the most part, the small homes were not quaint or charming. The majority of Wade's houses, the ones in which my friends lived, were simple frame dwellings, though each house, no matter how small, was graced by a front porch. Only weathering lent variety to their otherwise uniformly white exteriors. A few houses were bleached frequently; a larger number displayed a dingy white that signaled several years' wear; still others exhibited the motley gray of peeled paint that had been applied a decade or more before.

Decorative shrubs were scattered about haphazardly in the yards of the smaller homes: there were dogwoods in white and pink, crepe myrtles in a variety of reds, and perhaps a hydrangea or a forsythia. Their spring blossoms were brilliant against the village drabness, their foliage merging unnoticed into a ubiquitous green background with the approach of summer. The larger frame houses, like that of my grandfather, were surrounded by foundation plants, usually azaleas, whose banks of red, pink, and white lent a vivid, but brief, splash of color in spring. Green was the dominant color year round, the green of azaleas and camelias, of the longleaf pines in my grandfather's yard, and of the two huge magnolias that stood sentinel over Mr. Oscar Starling's home and into whose luxuriant branches my friends and I shot thousands of BBs trying to still the songs of the blackbirds that flocked there on summer evenings.

Only the "better" homes of the village had lawns, not the smooth green lawns of *Better Homes and Gardens* but lawns of several grasses and a variety of weeds, with the greenish-brown hue of army camouflage. Because my father had purchased one of Wade's first lawn mowers, I was hired to cut many of those lawns and came to know them much better than I wished. I hated them—the spots of sand that the mower blew against my legs, the sand spurs so tall and thick that I had to wear socks and shoes even on the hottest days, and the clumps of weeds that repeatedly choked off the mower and forced me to tug at the rope starter.

The dirt yards of Wade's other houses required considerably less upkeep. The women of the homes occasionally swept the gray sand clean with twig brooms. The brooms furrowed the soil, creating patterns resembling those seen in the newly plowed spring fields. Freshly swept yards immediately attracted the younger village children, who considered them giant sandboxes created especially for their play. The neat furrows disappeared as the very young made mud pies or sand hills, the slightly older children played with miniature cars and trucks, and the still older kids engaged in the time-honored games of marbles and hopscotch.

Despite Wade's size and the easy familiarity with which its residents related to one another, I learned early that differences of race and class, universally understood and obeyed, separated its people. The whites, I knew, lived on the streets that formed the perimeter of the village. Along those streets were located the post office, the Baptist and Presbyterian churches, the white grammar school, all the white-owned stores, and the homes of most white residents. The more affluent whites, including my family, attended the brick Presbyterian church at the center of the village. About it were clustered the homes of several of Wade's more prosperous citizens. My grandfather's house, a spacious bungalow with a wrap-around front porch, was located about three hundred yards behind the church. The brick home of Mr. Oscar, the railway depot agent and telegrapher, was the first house to the west of it, and David and Lillian McNeil, whom I called aunt and uncle although in fact Lillian was my grandmother's cousin, lived just across the street from it. As a county deputy sheriff, Uncle David represented the law in Wade, and his wife was the postmistress. Those of lesser means worshiped at the white frame Baptist church, which was situated in a white residential neighborhood just east of the highway. Originally a turn-of-the-century school, the building had been converted to religious use by a dissident faction of the Presbyterian congregation, a group, I was convinced, of individuals bored with Presbyterian sermons and hymn singing.

Most of the less affluent whites, like many of the blacks, worked at the sawmill. Some, such as Dobin Baker, a sawyer and my best friend's father, held skilled positions. Better-educated whites—those who had completed high school—were railroad employees, or, like my grandfather, local merchants. Other village residents were salespeople or professionals, as my father was, and held jobs or maintained offices in Fayetteville. Fort Bragg, a sprawling army base located next to Fayetteville, employed a number of Wade's residents, black and white, in a variety of positions. A few others held federal civil service positions or worked at the post office with Aunt Lillian. The handful of college-educated residents included the Presbyterian minister and the schoolteachers, all women from more prosperous families.

Most blacks lived in "the Bottom," a section of Wade I rarely entered unless accompanying my father or grandfather on a specific mission. The Bottom occupied a low-lying area on the north side of town, curving eastward from the railroad to reach the highway along the northernmost outskirts of the village. Here rows of dilapidated frame houses—most of which were owned by the Tart Lumber Company and housed its workers—lined the neighborhood's single dirt road. Automobiles navigated the lane at some peril and, depending on the weather, frequently stuck in either mud or sand. In the matchbox houses, where plumbing was limited to a hand pump mounted over a sink on the back porch, lived families of from six to twelve people. Chinaberry trees shaded the houses of the Bottom from a blistering summer sun. Their green leaves contrasted with the old whitewashed automobile tires buried in the dirt yards and filled with petunias or wild roses. On tiny front porches a rusty can or two of begonias blossomed, their coral flowers adding a poignant touch of beauty to structures whose every line announced the low economic and social status of their inhabitants.

Surrounding the village for a distance of some three miles in every direction were the outlying farms for which Wade was the hub. Because the farms were beyond the range of an easy bike ride, they seemed very far away and vastly different from the familiar village. Still, I knew most of the farm families personally, attended school with their children, and saw the parents in the village on rainy days and Saturdays and in church on Sundays. White families owned almost all of the farms, and most of the families lived on and worked the land. A few large landowners lived in the village; tenants, most but by no means all of whom were black, worked the land. I knew the tenant families, too, black and white, though not as well as I knew the landowners and the people of the village. Many of the white tenants, I soon realized, were little better off economically than their black counterparts. In subtle ways my family conveyed the message that the white tenant farmers were beneath us, although their skin color gave them a certain social acceptability. Whites who owned and tended small family farms, and whom my family regarded more highly, relied heavily on black day laborers. These blacks, who were always referred to as field hands, were especially evident at planting and harvest time, but many worked year round, finding a day's work here and there. The few blacks who owned twenty- or thirty-acre farms relied upon themselves alone to wrest a living from the land.

In both the village and the country, the laws and customs of segregation were rigorously ahered to, except that there was no geographic segregation in rural areas. The families of many of my friends lived next door to blacks, although next door might have been a quarter of a mile distant. We lived on the eastern boundary of the village, and while our nearest neighbors were white, several black families lived immediately behind us. Especially on a clear summer evening, I could hear the children playing and the dogs barking, and I could observe the comings and goings in at least three households.

Daily routine in Wade demanded that blacks and whites work together, encounter one another at the store or the post office, talk occasionally as neighbors. Yet early in life I learned, almost unconsciously, that both races observed the unspoken etiquette of segregation. Blacks who had to enter our house, for whatever reason, came in the back door. Unless employed as domestic servants, blacks conducted business with my father or mother on the back porch or, on rare occasions, in the kitchen. Blacks never entered our dining or living areas, or those of my friends' homes, except as domestics. Blacks, adults and children alike, called my father and grandfather mister; my mother and grandmother, miss. When a black person approached a doorway at the same time as a white adult, the black stepped back and sometimes even held the door open for the white to enter. The message I received from hundreds of such signals was always the same. I was white; I was different; I was superior. It was not a message with which an adolescent boy was apt to quarrel.

My great-grandfather, John C. Bain, had established my family's position in Wade's social hierarchy. A landholder who perceived himself as something of a gentleman farmer, he had also been the community's first mail carrier. The dependable income from the postal service had allowed him to move from the farm to the village, where he built a substantial two-story Victorian house in the center of the town. He lived the rest of his life in Wade, playing the role of village savant and dabbling in local politics, agricultural reform movements, and the writing of family history. After his death the family lost the house as the result of a series of unfortunate events. Some of our misfortunes were blamed on the Depression, but most were caused by the disastrous business decisions of my grandmother's younger brother.

My grandfather, known to his friends as Lonnie Mac, salvaged the family's social standing. He began his career as a yeoman farmer, and at first glance he seemed an unlikely savior. He was a short man, five feet seven at most, scrawny and small of frame. At no time in his life did he weigh more than 120 pounds. He had tiny hands and feet; before I completed grade school I wore a larger shoe size than he did.

Granddaddy's size was deceptive; he was as hard as nails, presenting to the world, his family included, a personality that was relentlessly stern, yet never uncaring. A bout as a youth with an undiagnosed respiratory illness, probably tuberculosis, robbed him of what my grandmother said had been a rich baritone voice. His harsh, rasping, high-pitched voice made him seem the more formidable. That voice, by its very uniqueness, projected authority and demanded deference, if not obedience. His steel gray eyes— intelligent, restless, commanding—compelled people to notice him, and whether they were friend or foe, he always met their gaze. He was shrewd and ambitious, and unquestionably life had made him hard. I always suspected, however, that he enjoyed the role of the tough little man, the hard-nosed, unyielding survivor who met life straight on, expecting no favors and seeking none. He married my grandmother, Alma Bain, over her family's objections and took her to a small farm purchased in part with money earned during a brief stint as a railway telegrapher. The farm was located on a stretch of river bottom land that Wade's residents referred to sim- ply and accurately as the Swamp. He was nearly thirty, she barely twenty.

My grandmother gave birth to my father in the early days of the great influenza epidemic of 1919. She was stricken by the virus herself, and for nearly a week before delivery her fever exceeded 104 degrees. Black women from nearby farms nursed her through the cold damp nights. My grandmother survived but never com- pletely recovered from her ordeal. Although the fever did not affect her intelligence, it so impaired her ability to cope with reality that she was unable to bring up the child she had borne. Before my father reached his fifth birthday, the farmhouse burned and his fam- ily moved into the big two-story house in Wade with my grand- mother's parents. For the moment, Granddaddy relied upon her father, John C. Bain, who from his Victorian sanctuary continued to work for the Masonic order, fulfill his duties as mail carrier, and champion what he deemed progressive political causes.

The loss of his home proved a stroke of luck for Granddaddy. Using money from an insurance policy on the farmhouse, he built a store and embarked upon his lifelong career as a village merchant. He constructed the store beside the highway just north of the city limits. He chose that location to escape village taxes and blue laws, and to give residents a Sunday alternative to placing their money in

the collection plates of local churches. His new undertaking promised an infinitely more prosperous and comfortable life than the
malaria-ridden lowland farm he had abandoned. The original structure was a plain frame building, its exterior pine planking painted
white, with rough wooden floors and elongated window casements
to provide light, as electricity was still a decade into the future. The
1920s were good years. The business prospered, and Granddaddy
built his own home, a substantial white frame bungalow, on a lot
beside the house of his father-in-law.

While Granddaddy's business flourished, his family did not.
There were no more children. For whatever reasons, and as a child
I never heard any expressed, the matrimonial bond between my
grandfather and grandmother snapped. Granddaddy drank heavily,
going on periodic binges that threatened the prosperity of the store
and would have destroyed him except for the loyalty of his close
friends. Meanwhile, my grandmother's behavior grew increasingly
bizarre. She refused to accept any household responsibilities; instead she arose and retired when the mood struck her, preparing
meals for herself only, to suit her individual schedule. In spells of
severe depression, she sobbed alone in her room, convinced that
no one loved or cared for her. Occasionally she wandered about the
village alone at night; at other times she lectured neighbors on their
need for salvation. By the end of the decade her behavior posed
problems with which the family could no longer cope, and she spent
the next twelve years in the state mental institution at Raleigh, the
capital city sixty miles to the north.

Soon after my grandmother was hospitalized, the family disintegrated. Granddaddy rented his new house to the principal of the
white school and sent my father to live with the aging Mr. John C.
and his youngest daughter, Olivia. Refusing to return to the home
of his father-in-law, Granddaddy added living quarters to the store
and resided there for the rest of his life. When Mr. John C. died
during the Depression, the old homestead and his landholdings
were sold, despite Granddaddy's efforts to save them. Olivia, the
baby in the Bain family, for years had been isolated from life and

indulged by her parents. Without the protection of her father, she was no match for the world of harsh realities. She retreated into a nervous breakdown and joined her sister Alma at the state mental hospital. Though she recovered within months, she refused to leave my grandmother. Ignoring the advice of the hospital staff, she cared for Miss Alma for nearly a decade.

When my father entered adolescence, his grandfather was dead, his mother and aunt were hospitalized, his father was living at the store, and his home was rented to strangers. He lived at the store with his father but boarded at the home of a schoolteacher. When he was not at school, he was cared for by Jim, a black man in his fifties whom my grandfather hired for that purpose. It was a period in my father's life of which I rarely heard him speak, and of which I still have no detailed knowledge. Granddaddy had little time to invest in the raising of a son; he devoted his energies instead to saving his business and his house, even though it was no longer a home, from the Depression. He came through the Depression by selling gasoline to the occasional tourist and to Clarence Lee Tart for his lumber trucks, "furnishing" supplies and provisions on credit to farmers who he prayed could and would repay their debts at harvest time, and encouraging the "trade" of the black community that practically surrounded his store.

My father, named Merrill for an uncle on his mother's side of the family, somehow survived the disruption in his family and the peculiar circumstances of his adolescence. He rejected his father's advice to attend college and make something of himself, and at the age of twenty he left Wade for barber school in Charlotte, the state's largest city. During his year in Charlotte he met Thelma Melton, the daughter of a dirt-poor South Carolina cotton tenant farmer. Bright and determined, she was the only one of eleven children to finish high school. Like my father, she had come to Charlotte to learn how to make a living and had enrolled in a business college. Before the year was out they were married. Their training completed, the young couple returned to Wade in 1940 and moved into Granddaddy's house. Within months of their arrival,

Olivia and Miss Alma came home. My mother, now pregnant, faced the almost impossible task of adjusting to a new marriage, impending motherhood, and the presence of two total strangers, one of whom could never be expected to assume adult responsibilities.

Granddaddy, meanwhile, remained at the store, making no effort to rebuild the shattered American dream—the family, the home, the image of the successful member of the community. That was gone, destroyed as completely as his first house, which fire had reduced to ashes. The store—its customers, the circle of male friends who gathered there each night, the salesmen who called weekly—became his life. He opened at seven every morning except Sunday, when he opened at ten. Every night he closed at ten, although business usually ceased about eight and the remaining two hours or so were given over to conversation with friends, the regulars who made the store a community social center. He took no vacations, except for the drunken binges that occurred about every six months and usually lasted two or three days. He had survived the Depression, but he had paid a high price for survival. He had become the indomitable little man, taught by experience to stifle any expression of feeling, to be emotionally tough and to cloak his caring with blunt speech and a hard, cold demeanor calculated to keep everyone at a safe distance.

I loved my grandfather, and I admired and respected his emotional toughness, his obvious intelligence, and his personal integrity and independence. Granddaddy cared little about what the villagers thought of him, although he cherished the respect of his friends and his reputation as an honest man. He was oblivious to fashion, dressing intead in a uniform of khaki pants and shirt and Florsheim oxfords, which he had cut to accommodate his bunions. He never entered a church except to attend the funerals of friends or family members.

Had he been Job, I suspect he would have cursed God and died. He had little respect for a deity who allowed the harsh circumstances he had experienced and the harsher ones he had witnessed. He detested radio evangelists, whom he regarded as a southern scourge and to whom Miss Alma sent hundreds of dollars after her return from the mental hospital. Her donations were part of a doomed effort to wash the world in the blood of the Lamb, and she considered them a small sacrifice to bring to the residents of Wade and radio land the sure knowledge of the precious Savior who guided her through a murky reality toward a glorious hereafter. Granddaddy viewed the media evangelists in a decidedly different light. "Goddamned phony son-of-a-bitch" was his favored description of such personalities as Oral Roberts and Billy Graham, at whom he directed his wrath upon learning of yet another of Miss Alma's donations. I quickly learned that to Granddaddy, *phony* was the pejorative word; anyone could be a son-of-a-bitch.

The Second World War brought my family a level of prosperity uncontemplated even in the boom years of the twenties, and equaled or surpassed by few area residents. In the late twenties Granddaddy had constructed one of the region's first motels—several "tourists cabins" behind the store. The military and civilian personnel that streamed into the area surrounding Fort Bragg created an insatiable demand for housing. Realizing an opportunity when he saw it, Granddaddy converted the cabins into one- and two-room rental units and turned a tidy profit. Increased wartime activity created more jobs at the fort and poured money into the local economy, and the store flourished. By the war's end, Granddaddy was successfully speculating in the stock market.

My father also made the most of wartime economic opportunities. A benevolent medical examiner declared him unfit for military duty. (He stood five feet eight inches, weighed 120 pounds, and had flat feet. All his friends called him Pee Wee rather than Merrill.) Aided by his father's financial resources, he purchased a four-chair barber shop at Fort Bragg. There he and three employees methodically sheared new recruits, a process that earned him enough capital to buy a second shop in Fayetteville. Mother, meanwhile, was occupied with rearing children. I was the first and was joined by a sibling every two years. After the birth of the second and third children, Juanita and Timothy, Daddy moved his family into a home of his own, leaving Olivia and Miss Alma alone in the house in Wade. Located on the eastern edge of the village, our new home was a plain but comfortable three-bedroom house. Daddy had obtained it when Granddaddy foreclosed on a long-standing debt. Two years after we moved, Maxine was born. Four and a half years later, Mother gave birth to Merrill, Jr. I would always wonder how Daddy knew Merrill would be the last boy. Six years later Mother gave birth to Renee, who completed the family.

Foreseeing that his opportunities might be limited in the postwar economy if he remained a barber, soon after the war Daddy became a part-time agent for a large insurance company. As if in compensation for a less than idyllic childhood, his luck as an adult was incredible. Soon after entering the insurance business, he obtained the policyholders of a cousin, Aunt Lillian's son, who left the company's sales force to enter management. One year later the state of North Carolina began to require all motorists to carry liability insurance, and Daddy seized the opportunity. A gregarious nature, a gift for gab, a sharp wit, and a desire to make money combined to make him a success at his new profession. By the early fifties, sometime after my twelfth birthday, he had sold both barber shops and committed himself to an increasingly profitable sales career.

Daddy's success in the insurance field further enhanced our family's social standing in the village. Our status could be measured by a number of factors, most of which I took for granted but nevertheless understood. None of my immediate family either farmed or worked in a mill. My grandfather operated a successful business, owned a "nice" house, and was knowledgeable about investments, which were as foreign to most of Wade's residents as Continental cuisine. My father maintained an office in Fayetteville, purchased a new automobile every other year (by the time I graduated from high school he had moved up from Chevrolets and Plymouths to Dodges and Buicks), and was active in local politics. The family maintained two automobiles, always had cash, occasionally dined out in Fayetteville and traveled from Florida to Virginia (but never into Yankee territory). Every year we vacationed for a week or two at one of North Carolina's beaches, an event eagerly anticipated by all the children, my father being the oldest. We dressed well, lived in a comfortable home with all the modern conveniences, and attended the Presbyterian church. (Wade was too small, too rural, and too Celtic to have Episcopalians.) In Wade's social hierarchy, we were "well off."

Like many such families in small southern towns, we assumed that the blacks of the village were in residence primarily to serve us, and we used their labor to support our comfortable lifestyle. Yet we never employed resident domestic servants, partly because they were more expensive and partly because they weren't necessary. The proximity of large numbers of blacks, many with no alternate employment available, made residential domestics superfluous. If Mother needed a nursemaid, or if she required help with washing, ironing, cleaning, or other domestic chores, she simply drove to the home of one of a dozen or so black families and requested the services of an adult female. If the person requested was not available for some reason, she drove to the next house. Within minutes she always returned with her help for the day. It might be Aunt Nancy, an ancient woman who lived alone in a small shack about a half mile down the road. Or it might be Dora Lou, who lived for a time in the Bottom, or Jeanette, who lived with her own family of four children behind Granddaddy's store, or Rheta, who lived in front of the store with her five children and husband. Our family expected these women to be available when we needed them, and usually they were. I saw nothing unusual in Mother's bringing home six or seven different women for a day's work during a period of a couple of months. The women were generic maids, interchangeable and cheap.

If the family needed someone to perform heavy labor—move furniture, haul trash, plow the garden, dig a well—we called upon a similar number of black men. There was Jerry, a retired farmer who lived in the small black community behind Granddaddy's store; or Sam, who lived in the country; or Alex, a tenant farmer and erstwhile preacher who lived about a mile from our house. There were others as well: Heck, whom my father considered too old and too slow; and Street, an itinerant Jehovah's Witness teacher, a prodigious worker but deemed unreliable because of his independence and his dedication to spreading his faith. I knew them all, saw them frequently in the community, and, until adolescence, simply assumed that they enjoyed working for my parents and grandparents.

At the store, however, I came to know blacks as individuals with lives of their own, not merely as domestic servants and handymen who passed through the life of the family. Working there I enjoyed close contact with them, not as equals but in something other than a servant-master relationship, or even a black-white relationship. More than most of the whites of the community, I associated daily with blacks of all ages, both sexes, and various social positions. Since the store was Granddaddy's life, he insisted upon keeping it open even after he reached the age of retirement. Committed to a different career, Daddy had no interest in maintaining the business, yet Granddaddy refused to sell it, and as long as Granddaddy lived Daddy felt the family was obligated to keep it open. Gradually, as Granddaddy aged, Mother began to assume major responsibilities at the store. As soon as I was considered old enough, I was called upon to replace her. From then on, though I slept at the house, the store was as much my home.

The store sat beside Highway 301, opposite the northern section of the Bottom. Granddaddy had replaced the original wooden building with a concrete-block structure some three or four years before I began work. Looking out the two large plate glass windows on either side of the front double doors of the building, I could see the houses of more than a dozen black families. Immediately across the highway stood the African Methodist Episcopal Zion Church, a simple white frame structure with a miniature bell tower over the vestibule, its doorway flanked by blue signs with white lettering proclaiming that "JESUS SAVES" and asking, "WHERE WILL YOU SPEND ETERNITY?" Beyond the church a row of six houses, all the homes of blacks, stretched northward along the highway.

Directly behind the store was another group of houses, approached by a narrow dirt road that twisted back from the highway through a stand of giant pines whose misshapen roots protruded from the earth to assault the wheels of passing automobiles. Unlike the houses of the Bottom, most of those behind the store were owned by the blacks who lived in them. Most of these people were members of two families, each headed by an older man who had managed, God knows how, to save some money as a tenant farmer. One home, a modest block structure with a fireplace and a front porch, was the finest black house in the village. Its owner was "respected" by whites for his frugality and upheld as a model for Negro citizens. Of course, he "knew his place" and, outwardly at least, displayed no evidence that he was discontented with it.

Next to the store on the north was the black elementary school, which housed grades one through seven. The rambling one-story frame building symbolized the status of blacks in the village. It had no kitchen; its students enjoyed no lunch program. Those with money came to the store at lunch to buy snacks and pop; others carried bag lunches; some went hungry. A row of privies on the back playground announced the building's lack of indoor plumbing. In front of the school was a sandy playfield, barren of grass, shrubs, and playground equipment. Sports equipment consisted of a rickety basketball goal and a makeshift wire backstop behind the home plate of a crude baseball field. The school served Wade's black children until 1957.

Less than half a mile to the south, near the village center, stood the elementary school I first attended, which also housed grades one through seven. (Older students, black and white, rode buses to segregated consolidated high schools outside the community.) A two-story brick structure, the white elementary school had been constructed in the early twenties after a local public education campaign in which my great-grandfather had figured prominently. The school possessed all the standard features of the day: a large auditorium and stage, indoor plumbing and modern restrooms, a well-equipped kitchen, and a large dining room in which hot lunches were served daily. A row of foundation plants enhanced the appearance of the façade, which overlooked a grassy lawn that sloped to a fence at the highway. Like Wade's homes and churches, its schools constantly reminded members of both races of their respective positions in the society.

At least half of Granddaddy's regular customers were black, many of them residents of the neighborhoods that practically surrounded the store. Blacks who lived on outlying farms, like many of the white farmers, "traded" at the store, coming into the village religiously each Saturday to buy supplies for the coming week. Teachers from the school next door stopped by after classes to fill their gasoline tanks or to purchase a few groceries or household items. At lunch periods and after classes were dismissed for the day, students swarmed into the store, buying candy and soda pop, and occasionally pencils and paper or composition books.

From the fall I entered the seventh grade until I left for college, I was at the store each weekday afternoon, each Saturday, and every day except Sundays during the summer. Every working day I talked and joked with blacks, waited on blacks, delivered groceries for them, and observed them closely. As "the other," aliens in my white world and natives of another world that was to some extent an alternative to mine, I found them much more interesting than Granddaddy's white friends and customers. Whites represented a world I knew intimately, one that at the age of thirteen I was beginning to find flat and boring. On rainy days and most nights, a half dozen or so of Wade's white males would sit around the store exchanging community gossip and observations about crops, the weather, or regional politics. Rarely were opinions offered on subjects which, by any stretch of the imagination, might be considered theoretical in nature. Their conversation, for the most part, was simple, a continuous rehashing of familiar subjects, none of which were terribly exciting to a young boy, who nevertheless welcomed any opportunity to be included.

Granddaddy's black customers, on the other hand, fascinated me because, to some degree, they represented the unknown, the mysterious. They provided a cross section of the black community. Among the men were the school principal, owners of small farms, masons, carpenters, preachers, bootleggers, and con men. The women included schoolteachers, housewives, farm women, maids, cooks, and practical nurses. I also came to know most of the black children of the community, boys and girls. I knew which black families went to what church, which had relatives in what northern cities. I knew the black families my father and grandfather respected, and why. I knew those black families my family considered beneath contempt. And I recognized which individual blacks, young and old, intrigued me most, although it would be years before I clearly understood why.

Because of my youth I could speak more freely to blacks, male and female, than could white adults. My age, to a degree, granted me an entrée into the world of black children and adults. To black adults I was no threat, at least under ordinary circumstances. Because I held no power over them, the fear that they felt when speaking to an adult white, especially one (like my grandfather) who had some power over them, was removed. Besides, it was natural in the segregated South for white children to interact with black adults. In some ways the white community encouraged blacks to supervise white children, even to initiate them into the folkways of the society. And I enjoyed talking to black adults. They had interesting things to say, and I was somewhat flattered by their willingness to converse with someone my age. Perhaps because they sensed my eagerness to be listened to, they responded to me, or so at least I thought. No doubt they told me what they wished me to hear, at least most of the time, simply because I was white and could never be trusted completely. Yet in the process they unavoidably revealed much about themselves. Because they did, my relationship with several older blacks took on a special quality, at least from my perspective. It was as if they despaired of ever leaving Wade, or of witnessing a change in the racist attitudes of the white adults of the village and the region, but wished that I, like the children and grandchildren they shipped north to the "promised land," could somehow escape the region's heritage of racial hatred.

That this extended period of close association with blacks came during my adolescence magnified the impact of that experience upon me. It came at a time when I had begun to question the values and beliefs of my society. My association with blacks would continue, as did the questioning, until I left Wade. A developing intellectual curiosity set me apart from many of the white residents of the community, not completely, but enough to cause me to feel different at times, and very isolated, sometimes enough to hurt. The whites of Wade, young and old, seemed satisfied with village life, if not with their economic status within it. They accepted Wade's social mores, its religious beliefs, its racist dogma. They resented and discouraged any questioning of their beliefs and values, especially from someone not yet an adult member of the community. Only the blacks I knew seemed willing to at least entertain questions about the status quo, and most of them only indirectly. Because they were different, outside the white power structure, and because they questioned its values, they, more than any group except my immediate family, shaped my concept of who I was and my hopes about what I would become. My appreciation of many of Wade's blacks as individuals presented me at an early age with the complex intellectual and emotional dilemmas of segregation. Before I left the village my association with blacks had also forced me to make some difficult moral judgments about racism and segregation. Those judgments, which most whites were so adept at avoiding, would further alienate me from the society in which I came of age.

Bobo

His name was James Robert Fuller, Jr., but everyone called him Bobo. He was a year younger than I, and I had known him all my life. He lived in a small white frame house in the black neighborhood behind Granddaddy's store. There seemed to be nothing unusual or special about Bobo; he was just another black boy in the community, of no more or less consequence than any other black child. Nevertheless, it was Bobo, a child I often looked down upon because of his blackness and his poverty, who showed me the emotional power that racial prejudice and segregation held over whites as well as blacks.

I knew his entire family. James Robert, his father, was a huge man, nearly six and a half feet tall, who appeared even taller to a thirteen-year-old white boy. He had the physique of many fine black athletes—long, thickly muscled arms, long legs sweeping upward to a short waist above which rested a powerful, well-formed torso. James Robert drove a truck for the Tart Lumber Company, making short runs to scores of hamlets in eastern North Carolina and Virginia to deliver dressed lumber to local building-and-supply dealers. He was a soft-spoken man with a gentle voice and blue-gray eyes. I remember his climbing down from his cab, his great long legs stretching to meet the ground, and I recall the easy, loping strides that moved him away from the truck. I also remember him drunk, for like many of Wade's poor male residents, black and white, he turned to the bottle to escape his problems, however briefly. Especially on weekends, but occasionally on weekdays,

James Robert would enter our store after downing more than a few drinks. At such times he was a sad figure even to a white youth: he was a giant to be pitied, his physical size somehow overwhelmed by the circumstances of his life, few of which he determined and most of which he could not avoid. When he drank he withdrew into himself, and in doing so he revealed his alienation from the world whites controlled—a world in which this huge man with smooth, copper-brown skin was just another menial laborer.

Jeanette was Bobo's mother. She had four children. Bobo was the oldest. Her second child, Jennifer, some two years younger, was a slight, timid girl with large mournful eyes. Two years younger than Jennifer was Chris, a small energetic boy whose black eyes shone with curiosity and intelligence. The youngest child, a girl whose name I can't recall, was an infant. Although Jeanette was still young, probably less than thirty when Bobo was twelve, she, like most black women of the village, had few skills that the society valued. In Wade there were not many jobs for black women, even for those who had completed high school or received some additional training. For women like Jeanette, who possessed little formal education, there was but one opportunity for employment: she "worked days" as a domestic, as did scores of her black sisters. For years she served a single white household two days a week—washing, ironing, cleaning, doing the heavy household chores. Other days she "picked up" work in the homes of Wade's more affluent families, including ours. She was a big woman, tall and long-limbed like her husband, already heavy in the hips. She did not strike me as pretty, although she had a pleasant face with nice eyes, a coffee-brown complexion, and an easy smile.

Jeanette was quiet, gentle, unobtrusive; all in all she seemed a terribly vulnerable figure. Yet she held her family together. She looked after James Robert, mothered her children, maintained the household, and brought home a supplemental income. When the family fell behind in its payments for the groceries purchased on credit from Granddaddy's store, it was Jeanette who had to beg "Mr. Lonnie" for additional time. Her supplications followed a cen-

turies-old script that was undoubtedly as humiliating as it was successful. It was a charade often played in the segregated South, a
drama in which all the characters knew perfectly their lines and
postures. This drama I frequently saw staged, several times with
Jeanette in the female lead, sometimes with other women in the
role. On the few occasions on which I observed a male playing the
supplicant, the script was revised slightly to allow the player a bit
more dignity.

The role required that Jeanette project an image of childlike
naiveté and innocence in order to deserve the beneficence of her
superior. When she sought an extension of credit or time in which
to pay her debt, Jeanette would ease into the store, head bent
slightly forward, eyes downcast, her face a sorrowful study of
helplessness, and with short, gliding steps she would move toward
my grandfather. Standing across a wooden counter from him, she
would pause and begin to shift her weight gently from foot to foot,
her body swaying almost imperceptibly as in hushed tones she pled
her case.

"Mr. Lonnie, I needs some things, and I ain't got no money,
nothing, Mr. Lonnie. I knows we owe you, and I'll pay you as soon
as I can, Mr. Lonnie, honest I will, but I needs some things right
now."

After her appeal was delivered, without noticeable change of
facial expression Granddaddy would turn and pick up his ledger
book from the counter and read from Jeanette's account. "Jeanette,
you owe me seventy-five dollars on this account. That's a lot of
money. I can't keep letting you have groceries without getting
paid."

Jeanette would then acknowledge Granddaddy's admonition and
continue to press her case.

"I know it seems a lot, Mr. Lonnie. But I'll pay—just as soon as I
can get the money. James Robert'll get paid next week, and I'll try
and get an extry day's work somewhere. We'll catch up, Mr. Lonnie. You knows we pays you when we can. But the children needs
some things now, Mr. Lonnie."

Granddaddy would then lay the ledger on the counter and shake his head, as if puzzled by the entire transaction and baffled by Jeanette's inability to obtain more income. Jeanette would continue to sway as she awaited his response, her eyes still searching the floor. After a long silence Granddaddy, like a judge sentencing a convicted felon, would deliver his verdict.

"Well, all right. This time. But no more than five dollars. Not a nickel more. And I want something on your account next week, you hear?"

"Thank you, Mr. Lonnie, thank you." Jeanette would snap her head up, stop swaying, then step smartly backward while bending forward slightly at the waist in an impromptu curtsy. "We'll be sure and pay some next week, Mr. Lonnie, just you wait and see."

"Well, just be sure you do," he would reply, and turn to me and command, "Boy, get Jeanette here what she wants—up to five dollars, no more."

"Yes, sir." And I would come to the counter to take her order.

I accepted such episodes and others equally demeaning to blacks as normal events of daily life, certainly nothing to cause concern. I assumed that James Robert and Jeanette and their family, and many other black families that I knew, always behaved in the way my father and grandfather, and most other white adults, expected them to. I knew, for I had been told since birth, that whites were superior to blacks (and for that matter, that members of my family were superior to most whites). On the other hand, I had also been taught that one should never mistreat a black, insult a black, or purposely be rude to a black. One was never to behave badly toward blacks, partially because of moral imperatives.

"Colored people have souls too," my grandmother, whom my brothers and sisters and I called Ma Ma, reminded us more than once. "Some of them will go to heaven with us." Ma Ma, of course, was bent upon getting as many people into heaven as possible. I suspect that she believed that white Christians would require a servant class in the hereafter, although she never elaborated upon her concept of the social status of blacks in the New Jerusalem.

Such moral considerations, however, rarely influenced the behavior of upper class whites toward blacks. The more compelling reason why one was expected never to abuse blacks—unless, of course, they acted in a manner that whites deemed worthy of chastisement—had little to do with the admission that blacks were fellow humans. Rather, it was because superior people never treated their inferiors in an unseemly manner. For example, one didn't say "nigger," not because the use of that word caused blacks pain but because to do so indicated "poor breeding." "We don't use that word in our family"—this was the standard response of women in our family to men who did use that word in front of children.

In the South of my youth "good breeding" was still extremely important. Adults who abused blacks "for no good reason" were held in contempt by my family, and as late as the 1950s the older generation talked disparagingly about whites who "treated their colored people mean," as if whites still owned blacks and were compelled by some social code to handle their laborers gently. *Nigger* was a word poor whites used, a term they hurled at blacks (whom the adults in my family always referred to as "colored people") the way my childhood friends from less affluent families hurled pieces of granite from the railway track beds at hapless black children their age or younger. Despite linguistic niceties, however, all whites knew that blacks were, really, servants. It was their destiny to work at menial tasks, supervised, of course, by benevolent whites. All this according to God's plan and was perfectly obvious to all but dimwitted Yankees and Communists. As a young child I could sit in church with the other white children of the village and sing "Jesus loves the little children . . . Red and yellow, black and white" and never wonder why no black children were in our group. Until I began to work at the store the thought that they should have been in church with us never occurred to me. It also probably never occurred to the adult church members, including the minister.

Race, then, was something I rarely thought about and never pondered—that is, until a single incident, a commonplace occurrence involving Bobo, made me aware of the tremendous impact a segregated society had upon my life. Unlike schoolmates like my best friend, Howard Lee Baker (named for Clarence Lee Tart, who owned the house in which Howard was born and in whose mill his father worked), or Linda Daughtery, the vivacious, sharp-tongued girl down the street who disliked me as much as I disliked her throughout adolescence, Bobo was never an important part of my life. Bobo was merely there, a child whom I saw frequently and played with on occasion, but who was of no real consequence to me. Because of his relative unimportance, because I had known him all my life, because he had been a part of my childhood environment in the same way as the trees and the school playgrounds and the dusty streets, because, like them, he had always been there, Bobo changed that comfortable, secure racist world for me. He did so unintentionally, yet irrevocably, in the fall of my thirteenth year.

I knew Bobo as well as I knew any black child in Wade. He sometimes came to our house with his mother; although Jeanette didn't work for us as often as several other black women of the village did, it was not unusual for her to be hired to assist with the wash, housecleaning, or other heavy chores. Sometimes she brought her children with her, especially on pleasant days when all the children, black and white, could play outside while she worked, freed from the distractions of child care. The children of the two families were approximately the same age and played together well, although even in play the special status of the white children was understood, if rarely acknowledged verbally.

Playing with Bobo and other black youths was a natural part of my life, and seldom very meaningful. Much of the time our play, especially team games and horseplay among boys and occasional displays of developing male prowess, involved physical contact with blacks, and I thought nothing of it. In my childhood physical proximity to blacks was natural and accepted in the society. If someone had told me that I could not touch Bobo because he was black, I would have been as shocked as if I had been told that Bobo was my equal. Neither concept was a part of the village mentality or of the belief system of the segregated South. Had such notions been proposed to me as a child, I would have rejected both, but as a child I never encountered them.

There was certainly nothing extraordinary about physical contact with Bobo. As a child I played football and basketball with him, wrestled with him, and competed against him in other games that were actually boyhood tests of physical strength. One such incident occurred when I was twelve or thirteen. Bobo, my brother Tim, and I were at the store. There were no customers, and we began to play a version of King of the Mountain. The object of the game was simple—to knock the king from his position atop one of the store's counters. The king, by bracing himself with his back to the wall and his feet pushed against a second counter, could absorb some stiff blows to the body without yielding an inch. Since I was the oldest, I was king first. I wedged myself between the counters and Bobo and Tim threw their bodies at me, pushing and shoving, struggling to unseat me. I could feel Bobo's body slam against mine, feel the competitive tension with each blow. He was a heavy child, not fat and, as I knew from encounters in past games of physical contact, not very strong either. During the contest I was aware of his blackness, conscious that his was a black body pushing against my white skin, but that fact did not concern me and I was not repulsed or upset by it. The game was short, broken up by Granddaddy, who returned and in unmistakable terms informed us that he failed to appreciate three boys tussling on his counter-tops.

We each enjoyed the physical nature of the contest, the straining of muscles and the measuring contact of young bodies, the sense of manliness that such exertions evoked. I had struggled to remain king to prove my strength, my power as a male, without any conscious understanding of a need to best Bobo because he was black, or to triumph because I was white. Such racial innocence, or perhaps naiveté, soon departed, and with its departure came the realization that segregation fundamentally affected everyone in Wade, whites and blacks, that no one was immune, and that it was a constant force, controlling our present and dictating our future.

The realization occurred in a comfortable, familiar setting on the playground. It was one of those uncommon common incidents of ordinary life which, because of some inexplicable turn of events or perhaps because of their timing, unmask some aspect of our life that we have always accepted as a given, place it in another perspective, and cause it to assume an entirely different face. Often such perceptions are not a result of either education or training but are instead mere happenstances, accidents of understanding, and are as unwelcome as they are unintended.

A basketball court was as appropriate as any place to gain some understanding of the larger implications of segregation and racism. In Wade basketball was the premier sport, played continually by boys, black and white, from September through May. The consolidated high schools, black and white, were too small and too poor to field football teams, but they could afford basketball programs. The goal of most male students was to make their school's varsity basketball team. On weekends the village boys played on the asphalt court of the white elementary school, a court that ate up the jeans and shirts and knees and hands of those who fell on it. Weekday afternoon games of one-on-one or two-on-two were contested to the bitter end on dirt courts, one of which could be found in the yard of nearly every house with a teenage boy.

Pickup games between integrated teams were nothing unusual; in fact, they were the norm when blacks and whites played on the same court. Teams composed of boys of only one race rarely played one another, because teams were selected by team captains who took turns choosing one player at a time. Since both captains wanted winning teams and since from years of playground experience they knew the individual skills of each participant, they selected the best players first, regardless of race. Although race was not completely ignored on the courts, it rarely influenced the conduct of a game. In all the years I played in such integrated contests, I never saw a fight provoked for racial reasons, though disputes over fouls, out-of-bounds plays, and other technicalities occurred with monotonous regularity during practically every game. The lack of racial tensions on the court probably stemmed from the fact that the society accepted, and in many ways encouraged, the practice of integrated play. Young

southern males had traditionally engaged in integrated informal
sports events, especially such outdoor sports as hunting and fishing.
Integrated pickup basketball games, as opposed to organized play,
were merely an extension of this practice. It was only contact with
females of the opposite race that was proscribed, and that only after
puberty.

Although my court skills were average at best, I loved the game
and played at every opportunity. I had a good eye for the basket but
neither speed nor height, and I was usually chosen somewhere in
the middle of the selection process. In pickup games in which Bobo
and I were on opposing teams we were often matched against one
another since we were roughly the same size and age. I relished
the chance to play opposite Bobo because he was no quicker or
taller than I and couldn't shoot as well. I knew that I could count on
a good game against him, and that I would score some points—a
welcome prospect for one not blessed with physical grace in an
adolescent male culture that stressed athletic prowess.

More than most white boys, I played pickup games on the dirt
court of the black elementary school. Games there were especially
easy to join on Saturday afternoons. Within an hour or two after
lunch several black kids would gather on the court and, if a basketball could be found, would begin shooting at an iron hoop nailed to a
battered and often-repaired plywood backboard. This "warmup"
would continue for about fifteen to twenty minutes, the players
dropping their best shots through the cords of the imaginary net
beneath the rim. During play the composition of teams changed
constantly as members were called by younger siblings to complete
some chore left undone at home or as players tired of the game. If
things were slow at the store, as they often were by late afternoon,
I could sneak out to join the play, sometimes with a white friend or
two who had come by on the chance that I could get away. Since
individual games were short and team membership constantly
changing, we could usually get into a game within minutes of arriving at the court.

One fall Saturday afternoon six of us were matched in a hotly
contested game, neither of the equally untalented threesomes able

to gain much of an advantage. Howard Lee and I, the only whites in the game, were joined by an awkward young black named Curtis, whose reasonably accurate jump shot was negated by his general lack of coordination. Bobo played on the other team, opposite me as usual. To a casual observer the game would have seemed thoroughly integrated, void of racial tensions. In fact we were unconcerned about race as we played, our attention focused on completing a pass, sinking a shot, grabbing a rebound. Yet the racial dynamics of this particular game, like those of all the other integrated games in which I played, were exactly the same as those of the village: the whites dictated the rules.

We were using Howard Lee's ball, which presented a challenge because it leaked air and had to be reinflated every thirty minutes or so. Since there was an air compressor at the store, I was charged with keeping the ball inflated. Although we played on a black playground, the white kids controlled the situation because we controlled the ball. None of the black players had a ball, so without us there was no game. Under the circumstances it made little difference which team won. However, had the black players challenged what Howard and I perceived as our rights on the court, we probably would have taken the ball and left the game.

We played into the afternoon, our play interrupted by frequent trips to the air compressor. When enough air leaked from the ball to cause it to lose its bounce and begin to interfere with the game, I would take it to the air compressor to pump it up. Some of the other boys, their game halted and lacking even a flat ball to shoot at the basket in the meantime, would accompany me from the playground to the store. On what turned out to be our last trip, Bobo and Howard strolled over with me as I went to inflate the ball. As we walked the three of us created brilliant passes and incredible moves with the flabby sphere, all of which we dreamed we would someday employ in the perfect game. When we reached the air compressor I pulled from my pocket the needle required to inflate the ball and without thinking handed it to Bobo.

The procedure followed for inserting a needle into a basketball had long been sanctioned by the rituals of kids playing on dirt and asphalt courts. First, someone wet the needle by sticking it into his mouth or spitting on it. Thus lubricated, the instrument was popped neatly into the small rubber valve through which the ball was inflated. This time chance dictated that playground procedure would fail; we couldn't insert the needle into the valve. Bobo stuck the needle in his mouth, applied the usual lavish amount of saliva, and handed it to Howard Lee, who held the ball. Howard struggled to push the needle into the valve, with no luck. Irritated by what struck me as their incompetence and anxious to return to the game I decided to inflate the ball myself. I took the ball from Howard, pulled the needle from the valve, and placed it in my mouth, convinced that my spit would somehow get the needle into the ball and us back onto the court. A split second after placing the needle in my mouth, I was jolted by one of the most shattering emotional experiences of my young life. Instantaneously an awareness of the shared racial prejudices of generations of white society coursed through every nerve in my body. Bolts of prejudice, waves of prejudice that I could literally feel sent my head reeling and buckled my knees.

The realization that the needle I still held in my mouth had come directly from Bobo's mouth, that it carried on it Bobo's saliva, transformed my prejudices into a physically painful experience. I often had drunk from the same cup as black children, dined on food prepared by blacks. It never occurred to me that such actions would violate my racial purity. The needle in my mouth, however, had been purposely drenched with Negro spit, and that substance threatened to defile my entire being. It threatened me with germs which, everyone said, were common among blacks. These black germs would ravage my body with unspeakable diseases, diseases from the tropics, Congo illnesses that would rot my limbs, contort my body with pain. Visions pulled from foreign missions films occasionally shown at the Presbyterian church flashed through my mind. I saw the white jungle doctor, Schweitzer at Lambarene, dressed in a white linen suit, walking among row on row of rickety

cots, each occupied by some wretched, rotting black. Those awful
African diseases, I now imagined, would claim me as a victim.

The tainted substance on the needle also threatened, in a less
specific but equally disturbing manner, my white consciousness, my
concept of what being white meant. Bobo's spit threatened to plunge
me into a world of voodoo chants and tribal drums. Suddenly the
Saturday Evening Post cartoon world of black savages dancing about
boiling cauldrons filled with white hunters and missionaries seemed
strangely real. I felt deprived of the ability to reason, to control the
situation. All threats to mind and body, however, failed to compare to
the ultimate danger posed by the saliva on the needle. It placed in
jeopardy my racial purity, my existence as a superior being, the true
soul of all southern whites. The needle was the ultimate unclean
object, carrier of the human degeneracy that black skin represented.
It transmitted to me Bobo's black essence, an essence that degraded
me and made me, like him, less than human.

I felt compelled to jerk the needle from my mouth, to spit it to the
ground and rid myself of the unclean thing. I wanted desperately to
wipe my mouth with the back of my hand, to remove with my pure
white skin any trace of this defiling substance. The urge to gag, to
lean over and vomit out any of the black saliva that might remain to
spread its contamination throughout my body, was almost unbear-
able. Yet I could neither gag nor vomit, nor could I wipe my mouth
with the back of my hand. Ironically, the same prejudices that filled
me with loathing and disgust also demanded that I conceal my feelings. The emotional turmoil exploding inside me had to be contained,
choked off. Not for a second could I allow Bobo to suspect that I was
in the least upset, or to comprehend the anguish his simple act of
moistening the needle with his saliva had caused me. The rules of
segregation which I had absorbed every waking moment of my life,
and which were now an essential part of my consciousness, demanded that I retain my position as the superior, that I remain in
control of the situation. More than the poison of Bobo's saliva I
feared the slightest indication of loss of self-control, the merest hint
that this black child I knew so well had the power to cut me to the

emotional quick, to reach the innermost regions of my being and challenge the sureties of my white world. He could never be allowed to cause me to deviate in the least from the prescribed pattern of white behavior. Thirteen years of conditioning in a segregationist society squelched my confusion. The unswerving assurance of racial dogma suppressed any instinct to flinch, any inclination to hesitate. Infuriated with myself because I had momentarily allowed a black—even worse, a black my age—to intimidate me, I grabbed the needle from my mouth and slammed it through the valve into the basketball. I jerked the air hose from its rack and inflated the ball to its normal hardness. Still angry, I flung the ball at Bobo, striking him in the stomach. Startled, he clutched the ball with both hands, holding it tightly against his midriff. He and Howard Lee glanced at me, Bobo's eyes filled with anger, Howard's with surprise, as each probed to find a reason for my outburst. No one spoke, and I met their gaze. Bobo turned, bounced the ball once, hard, caught it, and moved toward the basketball court. He paused and glanced at me again, this time his eyes expressing puzzlement rather than anger. Howard followed him. My white heritage defended, I stood and watched them walk toward the three black boys who nonchalantly awaited our return and the resumption of the game.

I had triumphed. I had preserved my status as the superior. I had prevented Bobo from guessing that his actions had destroyed my emotional composure. I had challenged him in front of another white and forced him to confront my claim to superiority. By refusing to question my actions and returning to the game, he had acquiesced in that claim, though he never acknowledged it. I had upheld the doctrine of white supremacy and observed the rules of segregated society. And I suspect that Bobo realized, as I did, that those same rules governed his response to me. He must have understood that he could not respond to my challenge because of who he was within the village social structure, and because we stood in the shadow of Granddaddy's store, in a white world.

Yet my vindication of white supremacy was incomplete. While I superiority and my right to that status because of , ι still felt defiled. The thought that some residual ...ation, some lingering trace of the essence of Bobo's black- ...ess remained with me became an obsession. I could feel his germs crawling through my body, spreading their black pestilence from head to toe. I had to cleanse myself—to purify my body of Bobo's contaminants and to rid my person of any remaining trace of his negritude. Only then could I fully reclaim my racial purity and re-store my shaken sense of superiority. And I had to do so quickly, without the knowledge of others, before I could return to the game.

I walked to the other side of the store, out of sight of the five boys on the basketball court who had begun to shoot goals at random while waiting for my return. From the side of the building protruded a faucet, used by thirsty ball players who had no money for Cokes. Bending over, I turned the tap and watched the clear, clean water burst from the spigot and spatter into the sand. I cupped my hands beneath the flow, watched them fill with the crystal liquid, then splashed it to my face, felt it begin to cleanse me of Bobo's black stain. Bending farther, I placed my mouth against the grooved lip of the faucet. I filled my mouth with water, swished the water from cheek to cheek, then forced it through my teeth and onto the ground. Tilting my head, mouth still against the faucet, I let the cleansing stream trickle through my mouth, removing any remaining Negro contaminant. I splashed more water over my face and head, then washed my hands and forearms. Finally, I swallowed a large gulp of water, felt it slide down my throat, and in my mind's eye saw it wash away the last traces of Bobo's blackness. My rite of purification was completed. With this baptism of plain tap water I was reborn, my white selfhood restored. I stood straight, shook the water from my face and hands, and walked back to rejoin the game.

I don't remember if the game resumed at midpoint, if new sides were chosen, or who won or lost. What I remember is an awareness that things had changed. I knew that Bobo was black, that he would always be black, and that his blackness set him apart from me in ways that I had never understood. I realized, too, that his blackness threatened me, that in a way I did not comprehend it challenged my most securely held concepts about who I was and what I might become. For the first time I understood that Bobo and I belonged to two fundamentally different worlds, and that society demanded that we each stay in the world designated for us. And for the first time I understood that segregation was not a happenstance, an everyday reality of no import. I realized now that segregation was serious, as serious as life and death, perhaps as serious as heaven or hell. I knew, too, that Bobo was unchanged, that I was still me, that none of the blacks with whom I played or worked were any different than they had been. I also knew that there was something very wrong, even sinister, about this power Bobo held over me, this ability to confound my world simply because he was black. None of it made much sense at the time. But the knowledge, the understanding that segregation was so powerful a force, that it could provoke such violent emotional responses within me, for the first time raised questions in my mind about the institution, serious questions that adults didn't want asked and, as I would later discover, that they never answered.

Street

O f all the blacks I knew in Wade, none fascinated me more than Street. He remains one of the most intriguing individuals I have encountered, and one of the few who possessed all the characteristics I most admire in people. As I came to know him, I learned that Street had an unbounded intellectual curiosity, a strong ego balanced by a deep and genuine concern for others, and the courage of his convictions. He was an original, a truly unique individual, a man of natural wit, intelligence, dignity, and unswerving principles. To a teenaged boy with a hunger to learn growing up in an intellectually stifling environment, Street was a godsend.

I knew Street long before I began working at the store. We first met one summer when I was about eight, in the way I met most blacks before I started working at the store. Daddy had hired Street to complete the job of removing a large weeping willow that grew beside our house. The willow's luxuriant cascades of green foliage resulted from its location near our septic tank. Its roots had penetrated and clogged the septic tank drains, causing the family considerable inconvenience, and Daddy determined that the tree must go. The older children applauded his decision, since the willow was occasionally a source of pain for them. As punishment for exceptional misbehavior, Mother often sent us to the willow to select the rod with which we were to be chastised. We did not love the tree.

Daddy hired Johnny to fell the willow. Johnny, a black boy of thirteen or fourteen, lived down the road about a half mile from us.

Tim, Juanita, and I watched, fascinated as Johnny began to chop down our nemesis. He hit the tree a few good licks, sending wedge-shaped chips of wood flying, and grunting each time as the axe blade bit into the trunk. I remember the axe rising and falling, and Johnny pausing occasionally to wipe the sweat from his brow with a forearm.

"This be a tough ole tree," he said, after chipping away half the trunk, and finding the tree still did not budge when he pushed on it.

"Look like I'm gonna have to call on Samson."

"What you mean, call on Samson?" I asked.

He stepped back from the tree and leaned on the axe handle. "Don't you know Samson? The one in the Bible, Delilah cut his hair?"

I was well acquainted with Samson, both from Sunday school and Ma Ma's religious instruction, which came straight from the King James text.

"Yes, I know," I said.

"Well," Johnny said, picking up the axe, "when you got a hard job, something you can't hardly do, you gotta call on Samson."

He lifted the axe high over his head.

"Samson," he called, "give me strength."

The axe came down, then up again.

"Samson, give the strength." Again the axe fell and rose, and again Johnny called on Samson. Within minutes the tree was down, and I was impressed, by both Samson and Johnny.

Felling the tree and trimming its limbs, however, was the easy part. Removing the tree's gigantic stump proved more difficult, and Johnny, despite further pleas to Samson, wasn't up to the task. It was at this juncture that Daddy employed Street and instructed him to finish removing the willow stump and convert the hole from which it was extracted into a small duck pond.

Street worked for days digging about the circumference of the willow stump. When his spade unearthed a large root, he would dig around it with a grubbing hoe, then slice through a good sized section of it with a single downward stroke of his axe. He was even

then quite ancient by my standards, in his late fifties or early sixties, a powerful slender man of about six feet in height with graying
hair, dusky black skin, and a muscular grace to all his movements.

I remember little about what Street said to us as we watched him
remove the stump and shape the pond that replaced it. What intrigued me about the man was where he lived. Ma Ma and Olivia
had told us he lived in a cave, down by the railroad north of the
village. I couldn't imagine anyone actually living in a cave, but I
knew if Ma Ma and Olivia said it, it must be so. They, like a number
of older people, were undisputed authorities on the location of
Wade's residences, great or small, among other things. They often
took me, my older brother and sister, and our friends on Sunday
afternoon walks, sometimes down to the Cape Fear River, about a
mile from the village, sometimes up the railroad for a mile or so to
the Old Bluff, an antebellum church that was the mother congregation for area Presbyterians but was now used only for funerals and
weddings. On other outings we would visit the homes of old black
women who had served Ma Ma and Olivia as children in Mr. John
C.'s house. One afternoon I insisted we visit Street's cave, although
I knew Ma Ma was not fond of the man and detested his religious
beliefs. To my surprise and joy she agreed, and she, Olivia,
Howard Lee, and I set off to find Street.

On first sight of Street's home I was extremely disappointed, for
it was not a cave at all. Rather, it was a large circular pit some
fifteen feet in diameter and about seven feet deep, dug out of a bank
of red clay. Street had felled small oaks and junipers from nearby
woods and had laid the logs across the pit to support sheets of
roofing tin that he had stripped from abandoned barns. Over the
sheets of tin he had spread several inches of earth, which grasses
and weeds had transformed into a thick sod. A flap of canvas cut
from a discarded tarpaulin served as the door to the cave as well as
its only window.

Street seemed delighted to see us, as if he enjoyed our curiosity
about his dwelling and the opportunity to show it to us. He invited
us to take a look inside, which we did. Howard and I entered the

cave, while Ma Ma and Olivia peered in through the doorway. Against the wall opposite the door Street had constructed a brick fireplace, on which he cooked and which he said provided more than adequate heat on the coldest winter night. A tin stovepipe carried smoke out a hole in the roof, but the odor of the pine Street burned in the fireplace permeated his crude home and its contents.

The cave's furnishings were as simple as the structure that held them: a kerosene lamp to read by, cooking and eating utensils, a field cot with blankets folded across its foot, a couple of trunks in which Street kept his clothes and his few other personal belongings, and stacks upon stacks of books. Books, magazines and religious pamphlets by the score lay scattered about the pit. They were stacked on the floor, on the bed, on the trunks, on any flat surface within the cavity. Never had I seen so many books and magazines in a house. Street had histories and biographies, works on mathematics and astronomy, discarded encyclopedia volumes, and old copies of *Life, Look, National Geographic, Time,* and a variety of other magazines. The magazines, I knew, had been discarded by Wade's residents, including Ma Ma, who was herself an avid reader. Later I would learn that Street read all these magazines and seemed equally enthralled by each. This cave filled with books, I understood immediately, was the home of someone very special. Although I would continue to see Street occasionally, it was not until I began to work at the store that I learned how special he was.

Street was a regular customer, for Granddaddy's store was nearer to his cave than were the shops of Wade's other merchants. He kept a charge account there, and he always paid his debts. He had a habit of dropping into the store, winter or summer, just before dusk, when most of the residents of the village were at home for supper. I was often alone at the store at that hour, waiting for Granddaddy to return from his supper, which he ate with Ma Ma and Olivia at the house in Wade. I welcomed Street's visits, for I liked the man and delighted in the tales he told and the ideas from the books he read, which he gladly shared. During my years at the store, I spent hours

and hours talking with Street, watching the sun set through the plate
glass windows, drinking in his every word.

He was born Clarence Eugene Street in the cotton country of
rural South Carolina sometime before the turn of the century, he
often told me. His father had been a tenant farmer, and Street had
known some hard times as a child. Somehow, though he was a bit
vague about it, he had managed to obtain a basic education. He
married early and, anxious to escape the spiritual and economic
poverty of the South, took his bride north. Like many young blacks
at the time, he hoped to find employment in the industrial expan-
sion that accompanied the outbreak of World War I in Europe. He
landed his first factory job in Camden, New Jersey, and then moved
to Newark to a better-paying position. During the war years he
made money, more, he said, than he could have ever imagined as a
South Carolina field hand. He enjoyed, too, the relative freedom
blacks found in the North and the sense that he could become
somebody. His dreams of economic security and self-fulfillment for
himself and his wife were cut short by the depression that followed
the war's end and extinguished by the return of thousands of job-
hungry veterans. When he lost his factory job, he and his wife
moved to Atlantic City, in its heydey during the twenties, and there
he found employment as a laborer working on the construction of a
seawall. Again Street prospered for a time, only to see his hopes
for a better life crushed, this time by the Great Depression. When
his construction job played out, he landed a position as a cook in a
candy kitchen. It was, he often said, his favorite job, and nobody
made better taffy. He pulled it himself, never used a machine.

Street was vague about what happened next. I know that he
liked the work in the candy kitchen but found it difficult to support
himself and his wife on his earnings. The northern promise of a
better life faded into a grim struggle for survival, and Street and his
wife, like countless others before them, turned to religion for hope
and comfort. Street, however, rejected the traditional doctrines of
the fundamentalist evangelical churches he had known in South
Carolina. Instead, he found the solace he sought in the Jehovah's

Witnesses. His accounts of his early encounters with the Witnesses left no doubt why he and his wife turned to them. The Witnesses accepted them as fellow human beings, not as second-class citizens, and promised them an eternal life of joy on earth, not in some abstract heaven. Equally important to Street, the Witnesses urged him to develop and use his obvious intelligence and natural leadership qualities. They paid for some additional education, exactly how much and what kind I never learned, and encouraged him to teach their doctrines to others.

Street responded to the Witnesses' commitment to the universal brotherhood of man and to their concept that a loving Deity was incapable of condemning his children to eternal torment, no matter what their sins. He and his wife became active in Witness affairs and began to minister to others in Atlantic City. Not long after they became involved with the Witnesses, Street's wife died; he never said of what, although it was a long illness. With his wife's death, the Witnesses became the most important thing in his life. Sometime in the late 1930s Street returned south to become a full-time "teacher" for the Witnesses and would devote the remainder of a long life to spreading their message.

I don't know why Street chose to settle in Wade; he never told me. He had no people there, no ties to the village. Perhaps the Witnesses assigned him the territory. Whatever his reasons, Street adjusted to Wade and its surrounding countryside and set about converting the inhabitants to the truth as taught by the Witnesses. He had taken up a formidable task, for Wade's residents, black or white, educated or illiterate, clung determinedly to a conservative evangelical Protestant faith, regardless of their denominational affiliation.

Upon his arrival in Wade, Street's first task was to find living quarters, no easy matter for a middle-aged black man whose religious views, which he felt obligated to share with all he encountered, made him a persona non grata in the deeply conservative black religious community. Street enjoyed telling how he met the challenge, and I heard the story on more than one occasion. On one of his early tours of the village he had encountered Oscar Starling. Mr. Oscar, one of Wade's more affluent citizens, was a gruff, bulldog-jowled man who for nearly three decades had presided as Wade's telegrapher and railway-station agent. According to Ma Ma and Olivia, who looked upon such activities as outright gambling, shrewd investments in grain and cotton futures had provided Mr. Oscar with considerable capital. Like many southerners, he had reinvested in land and had become one of the area's larger landholders.

While Street never said so, I suspect that, as an older black well versed in the social structure and racial etiquette of the rural South, he deliberately sought a white patron to help him solve his problem. Mr. Oscar was perfect, not only because he owned land and held a position near the top of the village's social order, but also because he was pragmatic and unsentimental, not impressed by the religiosity that pervaded village life. He listened to and was evidently intrigued by Street's heretical doctrines, which were invariably delivered in Street's entertaining style. Although as far as I know Mr. Oscar never became a convert, he admired Street's sincerity and tenacity, if not his unusual views of the true nature of Jesus and the hereafter. He rewarded Street by granting him permission to reside on an acre of land at the edge of a bean field about a mile north of the village.

"Yes, sir, boy," Street would say, ending his account of Mr. Oscar's generosity, "Mr. Oscar give me that land, say I could have it long as I lived, treat it just like my own."

And so he did. For a man as inventive and unpretentious as Street, an acre was all he required. Lack of funds prevented him from building even a small cabin, so he hit upon the idea of the cave. It was, he said, something he'd run across in a magazine. He would live in his cave for the rest of his life.

One of the things that most impressed me about Street was his insatiable intellectual curiosity. Street seemed to have a book or magazine on his person at all times, a fact which, of itself, marked him as an eccentric among Wade's citizens. Even as an adolescent, I sensed that Street relished the pursuit of knowledge not for some ulterior motive such as power or wealth, but for its own sake. Although he, like me, had probably never heard of Faust, as a truly religious person Street intuitively understood that the love of knowledge could become idolatrous. For Street, knowledge was neither power nor success, but joy, and he approached learning with almost childlike glee. I was impressed by and envious of his ability to retain facts, even after I came to understand that his limited formal education restricted his access to them. No scrap of information, however obscure or esoteric, seemed inconsequential to Street. Recently acquired bits and pieces of information, new ideas or concepts were shimmering baubles to be admired, pondered, fussed over, and played with.

Few things pleased Street more than sharing his knowledge, whether it concerned the life of Abraham Lincoln, the Witnesses' interpretation of the Bible, or the dimensions of the universe. He was awed by numbers, especially those so large as to suggest values beyond human comprehension. Astronomy fascinated Street because it raised ultimate questions about the nature of the universe and man's place in it while generating an unceasing litany of numbers that could stagger the imagination. In the gray twilight of a winter's day, Street often dropped by the store to purchase his dinner, a can of salmon or corned beef, and to pick up some bread and cheese, and stayed an hour or more to discuss the wonders of the solar system or theories of the origin of the universe.

Street would begin his discourse with an observation about the ordinary, about things people saw daily without thinking of them. "You know, boy, it's 93 million miles to that sun setting out there, 93 million miles, and light gets here from that sun in just eight minutes, boy. Eight minutes at 186,000 miles per second. That's how fast light travels, boy."

His lecture started, he would inject a note of wonder and awe, usually with his favorite phrase, "Just think about that, boy, just think about that." Then he would continue, "And that's nowhere, boy, no distance at all. Do you know how long it takes light to come from the nearest star? Four whole years, just think about that boy, light traveling four whole years at 186,000 miles per second. And they say there's billions of galaxies, just billions and billions, out there spinning in space. Ain't that something, boy, we live on this little speck in space, lost in all them galaxies."

Like all good preachers, Street invariably concluded with a reference to the Deity: "Just think about that, boy, think about a God who created all that, and who still cares about us. It's a wonder, like it says in Psalm 8, 'When I consider thy heavens, the work of thy fingers, the moon and the stars, which thou hast ordained, what is man that thou art mindful of him?'" Street's awe at the size and splendor of the universe would have thrilled a Carl Sagan, and it thrilled me. During the years I talked with Street at the store, he delivered lectures on Mars, Halley's comet, novas, the relationship between tides and the heavenly bodies, and a catalogue of other astronomical topics. Some lectures I came to know by heart. Amazingly, his factual information was always correct.

Street's interest was not limited to astronomy. Geography was another favorite topic, and Street knew where Afghanistan was, who the Berbers were, and the significance of Iran in the Middle East. He loved to quote statistics of major nations, especially China's. "There are 600 million Chinese, boy, and in twenty years there'll be more than a billion. A billion Chinese, boy, just think about that." Street could recite lists of the world's longest rivers, highest mountains, tallest buildings, and largest cities, substantiating his rankings with strings of numbers of miles or feet or people.

I suspected that Street was the most intelligent person in the village, except perhaps for a young Presbyterian minister who served our church during my last three years of high school, and the best read as well. My conversations with Street were the high points of my days, yet I knew that segregationist philosophy held that blacks were intellectually inferior to whites. Street challenged all the stereotypes about blacks that the society demanded I hold. It was his intelligence, combined with one casual remark, that caused me to understand how Street, and other blacks like him, challenged the entire system.

In one of our conversations, Street had commented on the high cost of tin. Tin, he announced, was more precious than silver, came all the way from Malaysia. In fact, he continued, tin cans weren't tin at all, but rather were made from strips of steel that were given a thin coating of tin. He pulled some popular magazine from his pocket to show me an article he'd just read on the subject and then rambled on to another topic. I rarely forgot what Street said, and I filed the information about the tin cans along with remembered distances to stars, the location of the Tigris River, and other such tidbits.

Not long afterward, a typical group of Granddaddy's friends sat about the store's large oil-burning heater, swapping stories about crops and the weather. Like most adult white males, they paid little attention to me. I was supposed to sit and listen, and to join the conversation only if and when I was asked. Like most adolescent boys, I yearned to be admitted to their circle and included in their talks. For some reason, the subject of canned foods came up, and I leaped at my opportunity to join their discussion and to expand their knowledge of the topic.

"Did you know tin cans aren't really tin, but are made of steel?" I asked. I was shocked to see my question greeted with amusement. So I explained, pleased to be granted even their amused attention, that tin was precious like silver, that it came from Malaysia. A chorus of laughter turned my pleasure to anger. Don't be ridiculous, I was told, everyone knew tin cans were made of tin. It was perfectly obvious. Why else would they be called tin cans? When I tried to press my case, I was halted by an abrupt "Who told you that?"

"Street," I replied.

"Boy, don't you know that nigger's crazy?" came the response, which prompted agreeing peals of laughter that cut my dignity to the quick.

I sensed that I was not to respond, that the final judgment on the subject had been rendered and that if I replied the laughter would stop and I would be dismissed with an even harsher reprimand. I was outraged that these adults, these supposedly knowledgeable men, had so contemptuously dismissed my observations, that they were so smugly assured of their own position. But the sheer anger that surged through my body was superseded by a sense of help- lessness, and I did not speak. In my silent anger, I understood that a "crazy nigger" and I knew more, thought more, and, most impor- tant, had more desire to learn than did any of my grandfather's friends gathered about the heater that night. Suddenly I saw that despite his lack of formal education Street's quest for knowledge made him their intellectual superior. Calling him a crazy nigger, I knew, wouldn't change that fact. At that moment my respect for the opinions of Granddaddy's friends slipped, never to be com- pletely restored.

My realization that Street was the intellectual superior of most of Wade's white residents did not alarm me, for I think I had known it for some time. The rebuff suffered in the tin can debate only forced me to admit to myself what I already knew was true. That admis- sion failed to destroy the segregationist beliefs in which I had been so well drilled, although it challenged them in a manner I could not ignore. Instinctively, my mind searched for means of explaining both Street's obvious abilities and the validity of the segregationist rationale. I developed one that, not coincidentally, was flattering to me. So long as I believed Street was unaware of his superiority, I could continue to hold my racist beliefs. It was as if I knew a secret, and since I was white, my knowledge presented no threat to the system. This view, of course, implied that I was superior to every- one, Street and my grandfather's friends included. I failed to under- stand that if Street was the superior of most whites he certainly must have known it. The cockiness of youth and the strength of inherited racist concepts prevented my reaching this conclusion. When I finally realized that Street was aware of his intellectual su- periority, that he saw whites as ignorant, yet another prop was knocked from beneath the framework of my segregationist ra- tionale.

I was probably fifteen or sixteen at the time. Street had come into the store early one evening, while I was waiting for Grand-daddy to relieve me so I could go home for dinner. We were alone; it was cold, and people weren't venturing out to shop unless they had to. As usual, Street struck up a conversation, which he soon directed into a discussion about Witness doctrines. The teachings of the Witnesses, he explained once more, were firmly grounded in Scriptures. Most Christian churches, rather than teaching from the Bible, twisted its words to fit the church's dogma. Too many clergy were false prophets, shepherds who knowingly led their flocks as-tray, although he allowed that some simply didn't study their Bible enough.

Street warmed to his topic, heaping derision upon the belief that man possessed an immortal soul, a thing separated from the body, and that God would condemn the unsaved soul to eternal damna-tion. To prove his point, Street resorted to a favorite teaching tech-nique. He would pose a question, then have his pupil turn to a verse in the well-thumbed Bible he always carried. He then asked the pupil to read the passage, which, of course, would answer the question posed. It was an extremely effective technique when prac-ticed on people who, like members of practically all southern Prot-estant denominations, believed the Bible to represent the literal truth. I had seen him use the technique with others and had experi-enced it myself on more than one occasion. Street usually began with a sweeping indictment of Christian ministers, whom he classi-fied with lawyers, gamblers, and others he considered disreputable professionals.

"Preachers tell you everybody got a soul, that your soul gonna go to hell if you're not saved. Tell you that the soul lives forever. The Bible don't say no such thing, boy. It don't say man has a soul, it says man *is* a soul. Look there, read what it says right here in Genesis 2:7."

He turned the parchment pages of his Bible, moistening his fin-ger on the tip of his tongue to ensure that the sheets of paper separated properly as he approached the selected scripture. Find-ing the verse, he urged me to read, "And the Lord God formed man of the dust of the ground, and breathed into his nostrils the breath of life, and man became a living soul."

"You see, boy, you ain't got no soul, you are one. And sinners don't go to no burning hell, that's just something preachers scare folks with to get money. They die, that's all. Just like God promised they would. That's what the Bible say, and let God be true and every man a liar. Look here, boy, read this." He flipped pages furiously, reaching Romans 6:23, where I read aloud, "For the wages of sin is death, but the gift of God is eternal life through Jesus Christ, our Lord."

"See, boy, that's New Testament scripture. But God said the exact same thing in the Old. What did God tell Adam and Eve would happen to 'em if they ate of the fruit of the tree of knowledge of good and evil? That they would go to hell? No, God didn't say no such thing. He told 'em"—he paused as he turned more pages— "Here, read this, boy."

I read from Genesis 2:17: "For in the days that thou eatest hereof thou shalt surely die."

"That's what God said, boy, and God's word is true. Trouble is, preachers don't preach God's word. They scare people, tell 'em monstrous lies, that a loving God gonna burn his children in hellfire forever. That's a monstrous lie, boy." He paused again, long enough to breathe a bewildered sigh, as if the thought of telling such an awful lie about God was beyond his comprehension.

"Preachers tell their people not to listen to me. Tell 'em I cause their soul to go to hell. Course they ain't got no soul, but they don't know that. Preachers don't want their people to know the truth, they need that fear to control their people, boy. The truth will make you free, though, just like the Bible says, 'You shall know the truth and it shall make you free.' That's John 8:32, look it up, boy. Preachers tell 'em I got a Jehovah's Witness Bible, that what they read in my Bible ain't so. And some people, white people, so ignorant they believe that, boy. They actually believe I got a different Bible, 'cause their preacher told 'em so."

Street fell silent in the middle of his session, slowly shaking his head, as if words failed him in his effort to express the appalling ignorance and prejudice of anyone who would believe such gibberish.

Timing his dramatic pause perfectly to allow it to take full effect, he continued. "Now you take Mrs. Heath," he said, referring to the wife of a white sawmill hand, "that poor woman, she believed the Baptist preacher, told her I had a different Bible. I told her, Mrs. Heath, bring me your Bible, we'll use it, and it'll read same as mine. She went in her house and got her Bible, and I showed her, boy, just like I've showed you, that man ain't got no soul, he is one, and that God don't burn his children in hell, that God promised that the wages of sin were death, and God don't go back on his word. You know what that woman done then, boy?"

Another dramatic pause followed, while I imagined what Mrs. Heath had done: chased Street from her property, summoned the law.

"She burned that Bible, boy," Street answered his own question. "That's what she did, said her Bible must be a Jehovah's Witness Bible too, if it say such a thing. Went back in her house right then and there and burned her Bible. Poor ignorant woman. Can you imagine people that ignorant, boy? Burn her Bible 'cause it didn't say what her preacher said."

From the tone in his voice I could tell Street pitied this ignorant woman, saw her act as irrational. I knew that he must see many whites the same way and that white ministers, who he believed deliberately misled their congregations, he held in contempt. Most whites, like most blacks, he viewed as ordinary folk, potential converts to his version of religious truth, reasonable people who, despite the teachings of their ministers, would at least hear him out.

I was stunned by the realization that a black would find the ignorance of a white person so appalling as to cause him to pity the individual. Even more shocking was the realization that Street's compassion for Mrs. Heath rested not just on her rejection of his teachings, but on a broader, more basic concern. He pitied her for her ignorance of the Scriptures that she believed to be God's word, for her unquestioning acceptance of her minister's assertions, and for her fears of a religious viewpoint that differed from her own. He pitied her not only because she was, in fact, an ignorant woman, but also because she was content in her ignorance. Street's pity, more than my awareness of his consciousness of white ignorance, forced me to regard him in a different perspective. I began to regard him as my equal, and in so doing caught the first inklings of the tragic waste of human potential he represented.

Street's religious views did more than provide me with a means of understanding his concepts about whites. They fascinated me in themselves, for they were the first challenge to the conservative Protestant orthodoxy of the South that I encountered. To me then, they were as exotic as the teachings of some oriental guru. It was not the tenacity with which Street held his religious convictions that intrigued me. An unswerving adherence to a biblical faith was commonplace in Wade, at least insofar as belief, as opposed to practice, was concerned. Street, on the other hand, differed from other members of the community who regarded themselves as especially pious on at least two counts. The first and most impressive to me was the willingness, even enthusiasm, with which he discussed both the biblical and philosophical underpinnings of his faith. To me that constituted an intellectual revolution. As a youth in a small southern Presbyterian church, I had been taught that the answers to all religious questions were to be had from the Bible, in which Ma Ma, a woman consumed by religious fervor, had instructed me diligently; from the Westminster Catechism, a version of which I had committed to memory at the age of ten; or from the Presbyterian minister. Answers from any one of these sources tended to be brief and beyond question, based on an appeal to authority rather than reason. Most lay church leaders greeted difficult questions, especially from an adolescent boy, with an ill-concealed hostility. Street, on the other hand, loved nothing better than a probing, freewheeling religious discussion, I suspect in part because such occasions presented him an opportunity to display his mastery of the Scriptures and his deductive logic. At fifteen or sixteen, I was also impressed by the fact that he welcomed my questions and treated them seriously and with respect. I was excited by the contradictions between the traditional conservative Protestant view and the religious philosophy Street held, which I found infinitely more rational and persuasive than the rigid Calvinism of my congregation.

Wade's residents, like most southerners, worshiped a jealous deity whom they approached with fear and trembling. Despite their Christianity, the God they prayed to was decidedly Old Testament. Not much advanced from the tribal God of the patriarchs, he was an awesome Jehovah of thunder and lightning who smote the wicked for their transgressions. God's constant vigilance against sin received ample emphasis in Wade's pulpits, as did graphic details of the horrors and torment that awaited the sinner. Had Jonathan Edwards entered the pulpit of any of Wade's churches, black or white, and delivered his famous "Sinners in the Hands of an Angry God," the congregation would have complimented him profusely for an excellent sermon, although the Presbyterians might have thought him a bit emotional.

Street's God, however, stood in marked contrast to the fearsome Calvinistic deity of my youth. Though he remained an omnipotent patriarch, he was also a compassionate one, and Street emphasized his mercy. "Preachers tell you God burn his children in hell. You know no loving God gonna do that, boy."

He would get personal to make his point. "Your father love you, don't he?" Street would ask, and of course I would agree. "Now, boy," he would continue, having received a positive response, "you believe your father would burn you to death, no matter what you did? Course not. And preachers, they say God gonna let the devil burn his children forever. Forever, boy, think about that."

Street would stretch out the word *forever* into four or five syllables, until it seemed the word itself would reach into infinity.

"That's blasphemy, boy, blasphemy to say God would allow his children to be tormented forever for something they did in just a lifetime on earth. It don't even make sense, do it, boy?"

I would be forced to agree again that, stern as my father could be, I didn't believe he would allow me to burn to death if he could prevent it, and to admit that the idea that an omnipotent God, supposedly a loving deity, would permit the eternal torment of even the most wretched reprobate seemed a bit repugnant. Over the years, Street's personal religious instruction began to have its effect. Without accepting Street's teachings about salvation, I gradually abandoned the Calvinistic God of my fathers, much to the consternation of ministers, Sunday school teachers, and my family, none of whom, except Granddaddy, offered what seemed to me a plausible rebuttal to Street's unsophisticated defense of God's basic compassion. Granddaddy's religious views, which he summed up with the brief observation that "when you're dead, you're dead," verified Street's viewpoint, although they were a bit more bleak.

Street also introduced me to the heretical doctrine of unitarianism, although not of the New England variety. To a youth already troubled intellectually by the doctrine of the Trinity, although totally unaware at the time of the historical debate over the subject, the concept that Jesus was unique, yet not divine, held a distinct attraction. Street sensed my interest, and in conversation after conversation mustered his arguments for the unitarian view. He acquainted me with the debate that raged in the early church over the true nature of Christ and culminated in the Council of Nicaea. He argued with exaggerated theatrics the case of both unitarians and trinitarians, invariably casting the latter in comic roles. His history lecture complete, he would switch to logic. The Trinity, he proclaimed, utterly defied logic.

"God gave you a mind, boy. Now how can three things be one? Either you got three Gods, or you have one." Street left no doubt that he believed that the logic of mathematics clearly supported an unadulterated monotheism.

He would then appeal to his ultimate authority. Thumbing through his Bible, he would declare that "Christ never said he was God, never did. You know what the Bible says, boy."

I would reply that I wasn't sure, and Street would proceed to answer his question, Bible in hand.

"The Bible say, Jesus was the son of God, don't say he was God. Jesus thought different from God. Look right here." He turned to Matthew and related how, faced with death, Jesus prayed he would act "not as I will, but as Thou wilt."

"That's what it says right here," he continued, preparing to deliver his clinching argument. "But that's not all Jesus say, Jesus say God was greater than he was, boy." He flipped more pages. "Read right here, John 14:28."

As my eyes followed his wrinkled dark finger across the page, I would read, "I go unto the Father, for my Father is greater than I."

"Uh hun," Street would exclaim. "Now don't that get it. 'My Father is greater than I.' That's Jesus talking, boy, ain't no preacher. Jesus said that. 'My father is greater than I.' Them preachers tell you God and Jesus and the Holy Ghost all one, all equal and the same. Greater don't mean equal, it means greater, ain't that so, boy?"

Having no convincing rebuttal, I would once more be forced to agree, hoping that later some church leader could supply me with a refutation of what seemed a sound biblical case for Street's interpretation. My efforts to find answers to the questions Street raised, however, failed miserably. When I asked questions about the Council of Nicaea, the historical debate over the nature of Jesus, or the scriptural passages Street quoted, I encountered anger, not answers. Only the minister had heard of the Nicene Creed. So I read early church histories and stumbled onto John Hus and Michael Servetus. I plowed through the Gospels, pondering especially over the meaning of John's Christ and his message of unity with the Father, and gradually I began to fashion my own answers. They differed from those Street proposed, and in the years to come education and maturity would alter them. Still, Street had presented me with new religious perspectives and forced me to question the collective wisdom of the community. He had taught me that, even in religious matters, I should use my mind. He had also, by defending his beliefs, heightened my respect for an untutored black who could hold his own against the village elders.

My admiration of Street was not restricted to his intellectual agility and his knowledge of the Scriptures. He was a first-rate

entertainer and a spellbinding raconteur. Street often prefaced a
lecture on the solar system or a discourse on the Deity with a literal
song-and-dance routine, abandoning the role of tutor for that of a
Bojangles, all the while retaining his natural dignity. Performances
inevitably began with Street pulling a nickel-plated harmonica from
his pocket, blowing a few notes, and musing about how he learned
to play the instrument as a boy in South Carolina. Perched upon an
upturned wooden soft-drink crate, rocking to and fro, his bare feet
tapping the concrete floor (Street wore shoes only in cold weather
and on formal "teaching" missions), he would play a few bars. Ade-
quately warmed up, he would pause and relate a story associated
with some tune, then launch into his rendition of it.

Street always played animated tunes, railway songs, riverboat
songs, hunt songs. He poured himself into his mouth organ, body
swaying, bending double and then jerking straight, head bobbing
and weaving to the music, his feet slapping out the beat against the
floor. When Street played a railroad tune, his body became the
powerful steam locomotive. His harmonica wailed out the engine's
whistle and the rhythm of the massive drive shafts that sent the
engine hurtling down the tracks. His hunt songs conveyed the fran-
tic energy of the chase as he sucked from the harmonica the baying
of hounds hot on a fox's trail or broke his playing to mimic the
hunter's excited call to his dogs. Street ended his concerts by
slapping his thigh, leaping to his feet, and dancing a quick jig. There
was for me a magic in his performances that always lingered, and
Street would let that magic hover, breaking our reverie just before
it began to fade.

He often yanked us back to reality by recalling some performance past, one conducted years ago on a train or at a tobacco
market on the streets of some small town, for Street had honed his
skills as an entertainer primarily to gather an audience to which he
could teach his faith. Stories about performances long concluded
were as entertaining to me as the original event, and they always
carried a moral. One of Street's favorites concerned his arrest and
trial for preaching on the streets of Dunn.

Street had gone to the tobacco market hoping to teach the area farmers who were there selling their crop. He obtained an audience with a hunt tune, then began to "teach" his message to several farmers who remained. He would ask questions and then leaf through his Bible to read the correct answer. The crowd grew larger, attracting the attention of a city policeman, who took a dim view of Street's unorthodox beliefs and hauled him before a magistrate for disturbing the peace. Fortunately for Street, this incident occurred during the Korean War, and two soldiers happened to be in the courtroom. Street, who acted as his own attorney, seized upon that circumstance to provide his defense.

"Yes, sir, boy," he would say, rising to play the role of defense attorney as he warmed to the telling of his story, "I looked right up at that judge and said, 'Your honor, this is a free country. The Constitution of the United States say I gotta right to speak, same as any man. These boys here, we say they're fighting to preserve our freedom, to preserve our constitutional right of free speech and freedom of religion.'"

Having made his speech to the judge, Street turned his attention to the soldiers. "These boys," he would continue, motioning to two imaginary figures, "they backed me up. Yes, that's right, they spoke right up and told the judge. So the judge, he let me go, told me not to preach no more, except on Sunday."

At this point Street always berated the judge, not for restricting him to teaching on Sunday, but because, he would announce triumphantly, "the judge should have known that the Sabbath wasn't on Sunday."

He inevitably concluded his tale by defending the Constitution. "Yes, sir, boy, it's a great thing, the Constitution. Gives every man a right to speak out, every man." In all the times I heard him relate that story, he never said "even a black man," but I knew what he meant. Street never lost a chance to teach.

More than any teacher I encountered at high school, Street was my mentor. Of course, he had tremendous advantages over my classroom teachers. He was an infinitely more interesting person, and his lectures decidedly more entertaining. I had known him almost all my life and, except for those periods when he was on the road teaching, I saw him several times a week. Most of his visits to the store concluded with a lecture or discussion of some sort, in which, no matter how brief the exchange, he managed to convey some knowledge or excite my curiosity. Street's ability to teach, however, did not result solely from his personality and capacity to entertain, or even from his store of factual information and his love of knowledge. In the end, Street held my attention because I admired and respected him. As I grew older, I understood many of his limitations and recognized the fallacies and contradictions of the doctrines he preached. Still, I continued to admire his individuality and independence and knew that he was different, something special.

As much as any person I met as a youth, Street was free of financial and social constraints. When introduced to *Walden Pond* I thought of Street, for like Thoreau he was a man determined to live without the clutter of civilization, to be dependent on his wit and physical strength and to follow the dictates of his conscience. He was the first black I knew who seemed to live beyond the confines of segregation's dehumanizing edicts.

Street earned what little cash he required by occasionally working in the fields. He worked only when he needed funds, not to satisfy the local farmers' demand for labor. In his seventies he could still harvest tobacco under a remorseless summer sun and keep pace with the male teenagers who made up the bulk of the farm labor force. In the fall he picked cotton or gleaned soybean fields that had been harvested by Mr. Oscar's combines. He pulled the bean plants and flailed them by hand, obtaining a few bushels a day and selling them on the local market.

Street used the cash earned by his labor to purchase the few manufactured goods he needed, mostly clothing. Until the first killing frost forced him to spend additional money on food, he grew his own. He was his own physician, making poultices of collard leaves for cuts and bruises and concocting herbal mixtures for "stomach disorders." Croup, colds, and sore throats he treated with a shot of bourbon poured over rock candy, and for other ailments he had equally exotic remedies. Sometimes Street would disappear for a month or longer, away on a proselytizing venture, but he always returned to pay his debts. Granddaddy never worried about money Street owed. "Street's good for it, he'll be back," he'd say, and Street was.

Placed beyond the economic control of whites by his self-reliance, beyond their psychological control by his intelligence, even beyond their physical control by his faith, Street was the freest man in Wade. While adult whites dismissed him as a religious fanatic, underneath their disparagement I sensed both respect and fear. I thought he was a marvelous man and didn't understand the fear until later, when I came also to comprehend fully what a tragedy Street represented. During a senior English class, as the instructor explained the meaning of the phrase "some mute inglorious Milton," it struck me that the phrase described Street exactly. Had he been given the education needed to develop his native intelligence, had society allowed him the freedom to exercise his talents to their fullest instead of forcing him to obtain small triumphs over racist beliefs through the teaching of a rigidly sectarian dogma, his contributions to the society could have been immense. That realization, perhaps, was the ultimate lesson Street taught me.

I saw Street for the last time in the late 1960s. I was in graduate school in South Carolina and had come home for a visit. He was standing in front of one of the local general stores which also served as the bus stop, awaiting a bus to take him to a gathering of the Witnesses in Fayetteville. I walked over and shook his hand. Our conversation was brief.

"How are you, Street? You're looking good, like you're doing fine."

He said he was, that he felt good. He still lived in his cave, cut his firewood, raised and cooked his own vegetables. He remained slender and erect, and still possessed a great presence, although age had robbed his movements of their fluid grace. His keen intellect still glinted in his eyes, and his voice retained much of the lilt that bespoke his joy of living and made him such an enthralling speaker. Only his skin, wrinkled, dry, stretched over his bones like ebony parchment, betrayed his age.

Not long after that encounter, I moved to Alabama and never saw Street again. Later, during one of my annual visits to Wade, Mother told me he had died in a nursing home, just a few months after old age had driven him from his cave.

Betty Jo

U niversally feared and publicly detested, interracial sex was, paradoxically, a horror that Wade's whites embraced, as did southerners everywhere. It was a beguiling abomination, nurtured and embellished by southern folklore, a subject cloaked in mystery and tinged with danger, spoken of in tones hushed or indignant, but always spoken of. Sexual relations between blacks and whites became both the ultimate temptation and the ultimate taboo, a symbol of both the reality and the futility of segregation. The constant possibility, or probability, that temptation would overcome taboo charged the emotional atmosphere of the segregated South with a raw sexual energy that, almost at random and without warning, discharged in resounding thunderclaps of domestic violence.

In the segregated South and in Wade, race and sex were so interwoven into the facts and fantasies of life, so embedded in the folklore, that residents instinctively understood their interrelated roles within the society. The myths and the realities, however, were often so divergent that only an act of will could reconcile the differences. The insistent denials of white southerners to the contrary, sexual contact between blacks and whites had been an integral part of life in the South from the time the first slaves were introduced into the region. And while most interracial relationships involved white men and black women, relationships between black men and white women were not infrequent. As a youth, I knew that interracial relationships were a fact of life because I knew people who were involved in them and people who were the products of them. As I grew older, I often heard them discussed, sometimes humorously, sometimes with fear, sometimes with loathing.

Sophisticated analyses of segregation, such as Lillian Smith's subjective explorations of race and sex or Gunnar Myrdal's objective sociological treatment of the subject, were hardly among the works read by Wade's citizens, even its most enlightened. I first encountered these persuasive condemnations of the system as a college student. Before then I hadn't the slightest notion that the conscious manipulation of racially linked sexual emotions, especially fears, was essential to the maintenance of segregation. Nor was I aware of the enormous amount of emotional energy expended by southern politicians and other leaders to achieve this end. The region's white male leadership, I would later learn from such scholars as V. O. Key and C. Vann Woodward, had developed an elaborate sexual politics, complete with racial stereotypes, which justified a patriarchal white-supremacist society. The society they created was one in which the collective id could always be unleashed to overwhelm the collective ego. Confronted with a serious threat to segregationist ideology, either from without or from within (as happened occasionally when the region's woeful economy became especially bleak and forced some to consider interracial cooperation), its defenders had a patent response. Segregationists resorted to the old reliable symbols, stoking the sexual/racial fears of whites, who, their emotions unleashed, crushed their opponents, often sacrificing a number of blacks in the process.

In the South's segregated society, sexual access became the ultimate measure of power. White males, who ran the society, enjoyed access to both white and black women. Black males were forbidden, on pain of death, access to white females. The issue of sexual access for white women was not considered. To do so would be to admit the reality of sexually aggressive behavior on the part of white women, a possibility white men generally acknowledged for black women only, at least publicly.

Both sexual and racial, the symbols used to manipulate the behavior of whites were projections of white male fantasies. To a large degree, they represented sexual desires condemned by a fundamentalist Protestant culture, yet simultaneously encouraged by access to black females. The white male culture, or at least part of it, invited me as an adolescent to share these symbols at a time when I was eager to do so.

By far the most powerful of the South's sexual/racial symbols was the Black Rapist. He was created in part from the stories white males told about his sexual prowess, stories I often heard.

"You see old John over there, boy?" I recall one of my father's friends, a carpenter in the village, asking me one day. "Now, he don't look like much, does he? I mean, he don't look like no ladies' man, would you say?"

"No," I replied, "he doesn't." And he didn't; at least he didn't fit my ill-defined image of a ladies' man. John was about fifty then, graying, a tall, lanky, slow-spoken tenant farmer.

"Well, boy, that just goes to show you that looks can be deceiving. They say that old devil's got a dick a foot long. Has to fuck with a washer around it. Drives them nigger women wild, that's what they say. Them women practically stand in line to get some of it."

The Black Rapist, however, was not merely a man of tremendous sexual abilities. He was a beast with unrestrained sexual appetites. The Black Rapist personified the white man's belief, and his fear, that the secret desire of every black male was to ravish every white female. He was, in essence, a monster created from the sexual desires of whites, desires that their religion pronounced bestial and evil. Obviously such a dangerous creature had to be controlled, his passions kept in check. The segregation of the races by sex provided the basic control mechanism and was a cornerstone of segregationist ideology. When sexual segregation failed to restrain the Black Rapist, however, whites resorted to violence without hesitation or regret.

In Wade, as in other southern communities, the Black Rapist was not just an abstract symbol. Rather, he was personified by some particular black man or men, a black considered especially ugly, one with known emotional problems, or one thought violent or "uppity."

Whispers about the barbaric acts of which they were capable, warnings about leaving white girls or women alone in their presence were commonplace in casual conversation.

"I can't help it," Mother would say, "I can't stand the man. He's so ugly he frightens me."

Mother's friends made the same type of remarks. "That Roger Eason, he's a mean-looking nigger," or "Just looking at John Wesley gives me the shivers. I just don't want him around when there's no one else at home. It makes me nervous."

I heard such comments before I knew what they meant. Years later, as an adult, I would hear them reverberating through political campaigns in Alabama as late as the mid-1970s, when a concerned voice in a radio commercial asked the Alabama white man if he would want a black highway patrolman to stop his wife on a lonesome highway at night.

Complementing the Black Rapist was the White Virgin, the Southern Belle, the "flower of Southern womanhood." Weak and defenseless, she was incapable of defending her virtue against the potential onslaught of hordes of Black Rapists without, of course, the intervention of the masterful white male. The symbol of the White Virgin was incredibly powerful because she, too, was personified by a specific woman or women. As her virginity was symbolic, the Southern Belle could be any woman: a wife, a sister, an aunt, the woman next door. Hearing women express fears of attacks by blacks was a normal part of my life, not something that happened every day, but something I did not find strange or unusual. Little girls were warned to "watch out for so-and-so." Older ones were admonished not to venture into black neighborhoods. "Don't you go there alone, you hear. You make sure you take somebody with you." Women and girls had to be concerned about their dress in the presence of black males. Shorts, for example, were forbidden if a white woman was to be near black men, because it was believed they could arouse the blacks' animal lust beyond the point of control.

On yet another level, the entire white South was personified as an unblemished virgin, threatened by the Negro's insatiable sexual desires. When my grandparents or their friends spoke of the South being violated during the Civil War and Reconstruction, and they often did, the sexual images of the Black Rapist and the Southern Belle immediately leaped to mind.

Of course, I didn't comprehend the South's erotic politics while I was in Wade. At the time I was far more concerned with the relationship between sex and the region's fundamentalist Christianity. In the neo-Calvinist theology adhered to by most of Wade's citizens, the cause of man's (and woman's) fall from grace was located in the erogenous zones. Southern Protestants regarded a healthy sexual appetite as the surest sign of man's bestial nature and fought a valiant and unceasing fight to vanquish their libidos. As I was developing an urgently healthy libido of my own, I was reassured to learn that the battle was frequently lost and that illicit sex remained a favored recreational activity.

Both races accepted these same religious concepts about sex (although it must be admitted that whites were the more stringent in their interpretations), especially the doctrine that any sex outside marriage was sinful. Since all interracial sex was outside the marriage vows (the marriage of interracial couples being illegal), those who so sinned were placed under an inescapable and crushing burden of guilt. Such couples were, in a very real sense, doubly damned, although whites believed some sinners were more damned than others. This was especially true, I quickly understood, of white females and black males, both of whom sinned simultaneously against God and against the white race.

Such sinners, I learned from an incident that occurred in my early teens, were believed to deserve violent and immediate retribution. A white farmer who suspected his wife of having an affair with a Negro tenant followed her to a night rendezvous at one of his barns and waited until the lovers were engaged in their forbidden activity. The farmer then calmly walked in and blasted them into eternity with a double-barreled shotgun. He was arrested and tried within a brief period, and the trial created a sensation. The man, naturally, was acquitted. What impressed me most about the entire incident, however, was not the man's acquittal, which practically everyone predicted, but the comments of the friends of Daddy and Granddaddy who gathered each afternoon at the store and discussed the trial's progress.

"The oversexed nigger-loving bitch got what she deserved."

"I can just see 'em humping up a storm. I'll bet that nigger turned white when he saw that twelve-gauge."

"Seems like a high price to pay for a piece of pussy, but a nigger should know better."

No one suggested that the husband should have been found guilty, "considering the circumstances." Indeed, the public seemed outraged that a trial was deemed necessary.

Black females involved with males of either race, on the other hand, received little condemnation from the store's informal court. They were simply following their natural instincts. The women were black, after all, and therefore were believed to possess insatiable sexual desires as well as incredible procreative capabilities. Unlike black males, however, they were allowed, even encouraged, to give their supposedly animal lusts free rein. Thus it logically followed that white males involved with black women could be forgiven for succumbing to the sensual charms of a Negro temptress. Again, the casual remarks of white males overheard at the store conveyed the appropriate message.

"That nigger'll fuck anything that walks, boy."

"Half the damned nigger women in this town's pregnant. That's the thing they do best, I reckon, have younguns."

"Niggers breed like rabbits, son. Ain't no way white folks gonna keep up with 'em."

Experiencing adolescence in a society so permeated with prejudice and passion insured that my pubescent mind was assailed by a barrage of racially linked sexual stimuli. The casual conversation of white men was easily the most constant stimulus to which I was exposed. Gathered about the heater in Granddaddy's store, waiting their turn to be shorn at the local barber shop (which opened on

Friday nights and Saturdays), or standing on a lawn on a Sunday afternoon, four or five in a semicircle with their backs turned to an automobile recently purchased by one of their number, their conversations were full of racial and sexual remarks and observations.

Occasionally a verbally inventive man would enliven the conversation with an original racial or sexual metaphor, but for the most part Wade's males talked in clichés, voicing once again lines handed from father to son for generations of southerners. Their lines required little thought; their responses came automatically—a guffaw, a hitching up of a trouser leg, a pawing of feet in the dirt. Some routines were as standardized as any found on a burlesque stage. For example, the query "How do you like your coffee?" was often followed by the response "The way I like my women—hot, sweet, and black." "The darker the meat, the sweeter the bone," was a favorite observation about darker-skinned black women.

The sexual prowess of black women had even been integrated into folk medicine. "You know how to cure that fever blister, boy?" one of Daddy's friends once asked upon noting a large sore on my upper lip.

"No sir," I answered, expecting to receive some practical advice about how to get rid of a bothersome and painful blister.

"Well, boy," came the reply, "all you gotta do is fuck a red-headed nigger. Course," he laughed, "first you gotta find one."

White males enjoyed commenting about the sex appeal and sexual activity of black women, predictable conversation topics upon the arrival of an attractive black woman at the store. Black women were the constant subject of rumor and innuendo, and for what passed as humor. Their sexual exploits and charms, whether they were married or single, occupied a substantial portion of white men's conversation. Such patter was invariably addressed to other white males, and all such remarks were kept low enough not to be overheard by the woman or women whose presence prompted them. The women, however, could hardly avoid sensing something of the general nature of the subdued male conversations, or knowing the manner in which they were being considered.

With the departure of a black woman, her admirers became bolder, their comments louder and more aggressive.

"Look at those tits that nigger woman's got on her, would you," or "Man, that's some fine looking ass," someone would remark within minutes of her departure.

"Wouldn't mind having a bit of that myself," was an observation I often heard, followed by some expression that recognized that such sentiments were not officially sanctioned by the segregationist code. "You know what they say, boy. The black don't rub off on you."

Initial observations sometimes elicited equally witty remarks from others in the group. The men would elaborate on what they would like to do with the particular woman under consideration. These male conversations usually followed the curious rules of segregation, just as did activities in other areas of village life. For example, appreciation of the sexual charms of white females, married or single, was expressed in "acceptable" language. Overt references about imagined sexual relations with white women, especially married women, were rare, however. White males also recognized the significance of marriage for black women from "well thought of" families. Instead of drawing a graphic verbal picture of how they would like to assault such a woman sexually, they imagined how her husband did so. Black women from less "respected" families, married or single, were afforded not even this concession.

To be perfectly honest, Granddaddy and Daddy rarely engaged in such masculine bravado. Within my family the expectations of sexual behavior countered the sexual contempt with which many white males regarded black females. Though never explicitly communicated to me by either my parents or my grandparents, the family's expectations concerning my sexual behavior were clear. I was to abstain, and above all, after puberty I was expected to avoid entirely social contact with black females. That expectation, and its significance, were made clear to me at about age fifteen.

My fuller understanding of Wade's racial/sexual mores was the product of an infatuation with Charlotte Humphries, a local girl of

my age. Impressed by her blue eyes, blond hair, and ample bust-
line, I expressed an interest in dating her, without, of course, revealing my less than platonic motives. Charlotte had been a school-
mate of mine since the first grade. I had attended her parties,
danced with her at school dances, played with her on Sunday school
picnics. Her family had been in the community for nearly fifty
years, so I was surprised and disappointed when Mother informed
me that it wouldn't be a good idea for me to date Charlotte.

"Why?" I asked, my hopes of sexual conquest threatened by her
negative reaction. I simply couldn't imagine why Mother would object to Charlotte, but I knew she must have a fairly serious reason.

"Talk with your grandmother," was the only answer Mother
would give, and so I did.

Ma Ma and Olivia were the unofficial family historians and gen-
ealogists, and we children were accustomed to being referred to
them about any problem with origins in the relatively distant past.
They were the keepers of secrets, the protectors of the family
name. They knew who had lived where, and for how long. They
knew the bloodlines of every family in the community—which were
pure and which weren't, when the impure were contaminated and
by whom. So I found Ma Ma and addressed my question to her.

"Well child," she began, "you just shouldn't. You never can tell
how these things will end up; it's just best you shouldn't, that's all."

"But why?" I persisted, not about to give up on Charlotte so
easily.

"It goes back a long time, son." She began, then hesitated, trying to determine how much to tell me.

"You know Charlotte's granddaddy, Mr. Walter," she asked, de-
ciding to reveal her knowledge to me.

I nodded. Of course I did. Mr. Walter Mathis was a small, quick
man with olive skin and receding wavy black hair whom I'd never
seen without exactly one quarter of a well-chewed cigar protruding
from his mouth.

"His daddy, Mr. Frank, came to Wade when Olivia and I were
just girls, about fourteen or so I was. Mr. Frank was a fine-looking

man, a dark, handsome man. Of course, no one thought much about it at the time. Family said they were from somewhere up close to Virginia, near Summerville. Walter went to school with me and Olivia, married Lottie Sessoms, one of our best friends. Well, about five years later, Ed Brown—he worked with the railroad, all the Brown boys did, Ed was a brakeman—he was in Summerville, and he asked about Walter. Mr. Frank was dead by then. He died a young man, can't remember how."

For a moment Ma Ma tried to remember why Mr. Frank died, then decided it wasn't important and continued her story.

"People up there said yes, Walter had lived in Summerville, his grandmother still did. She was ancient, over ninety, they said, lived out on the edge of town. Ed, he went and found the old woman. She was a mulatto nigra, a high yellow. Ed learned her daddy was a prominent white man from the community, her mother, a mulatto, had been employed by the white family. That's why they moved, Mr. Frank's family, so they could pass. Some of them do that, you know, son, pass for white, if they're light enough. Isn't right, of course, but you really can't blame them. Sometimes it can't be helped."

Her story finished, she remained silent for a moment, and so did I. I didn't need to ask what her tale had to do with Charlotte.

"It's in their blood, son, can't be helped. I know Charlotte's got blue eyes and blond hair," Ma Ma continued, anticipating any rebuttals that I might propose.

"That's from her daddy's side. He wasn't from Wade, you know, left Maggie when he found out about her folks. I hate it for the children but maybe it's for the best. You know Mary Ann, Maggie's oldest sister, she married a Strickland from Vander."

Vander was a community ten miles east of Wade, yet that short distance placed it beyond the ties of church, place, and family that bound Wade's citizenry.

"Mary Ann was fairer than Maggie, but her children, they're dark. Boy and a girl, both of 'em real dark. They say they have kinky hair, flat noses. It's in the blood, son, and it'll be there for generations. Now Charlotte's a nice girl, and you treat her with respect. And don't you mention what I've just told you, not to anyone. Still, there's no reason to start something that might come to no good."

With that pronouncement she closed the subject; the history lesson was concluded. I was left to ponder who Charlotte should date if she were white, but not white enough. And why, when the community learned of Mr. Frank's ancestry, the family continued to be accepted as white. I sensed that Mr. Walter's marriage to Miss Lottie had confirmed his newly gained white status while condemning his offspring to second-class white citizenship. I never dated Charlotte, and every time I saw her afterward, I thought of her mulatto great-grandmother and the white man who sired her, six generations into the past which united all southerners, and in which, to some extent, all still lived.

This revelation removed Charlotte from the ranks of Wade's white female adolescent population, a group whose numbers I already considered woefully small. As fate would have it, the number of black teenage girls in the community was tantalizingly large. This forbidden pool of maturing females contained tall, stately, slender, and willowy young women and short, stocky girls utterly lacking in grace; ebony-skinned girls and girls with the rich skin tones of dark mahogany; classical high yellow girls, those mulattoes who fill the pages of southern fiction, their long dark hair framing complexions so smooth they begged to be touched. There were girls with tightly curled, corn-rowed hair and girls with thick wavy jet black hair, glistening in the sun; girls with green and hazel eyes, brown-eyed girls and girls with mirror-surfaced eyes of onyx that looked at once through you and past you.

Since most lived close to the store, I saw some of the group almost daily, others several times a week. Unlike the white girls, who lived farther from the store and were rarely customers (perhaps their parents feared they would be raped by a black if allowed to walk to the store alone) the black girls came in groups, in couples, and alone. They came after school to buy snacks or school

supplies. They came on errands for the family, walking from nearby
homes to buy a loaf of bread or a carton of milk for supper, or some
other immediately needed household item. In the summer, sometimes twice a day, they came to purchase soda pop, ice cream, and
candy. They came to watch friends make purchases, or just to see
if friends were there, and to be seen by them. They were constantly in and out of the store, a parade of youthful femininity, each
girl alive with energy and sexuality. They were the stuff that teenage male sexual fantasies were made of, and I made excellent and
extensive use of the material.

My first fantasy conquest, however, was not one of the black
girls of the community but a black woman, perhaps six years older
than I. Jesse Florence McAllister was the oldest of three sisters.
At fourteen I thought she was about the sexiest woman I had ever
seen—certainly the sexiest I had ever seen in person. She lived in
one of the homes along the highway north of the store and worked
as a practical nurse in a Fayetteville hospital. She was married,
although I have conveniently forgotten her husband, and had a
young son. Jessie Florence rode a Trailways bus to and from work,
and often on return trips she disembarked at the store for some
last-minute shopping before walking home. Many a late afternoon I
wondered what time she would come in, or if she would come in at
all.

Jessie Florence wore her sexuality well. She was aware of her
physical attractiveness, was comfortable with it, and expected to be
noticed for it, the way well-dressed women expect their clothes to
be admired, even when the admiration is expressed only by a glance,
a nod of the head, or a momentary lowering of voices. Her voice was
pleasant and soft, almost too soft, and I never heard her raise it in
anger. She always seemed happy, her hazel-brown eyes reflecting a
look of friendly amusement, her mouth turned up slightly at the
corners in a genuine smile. She derived all of her considerable sensuality from the dual qualities of strength and vulnerability she projected; even her body seemed at once strong and firm, yet invitingly
soft, even fragile. She was a short woman, no more than five feet,

three inches. Compactly built, she had beautifully proportioned limbs, firm and strong, and marvelously rounded hips whose movement was accentuated by the snug fit of her white uniform, whose ability to caress, to linger over those beautifully formed buttocks, I so envied. The V of her starched white blouse invariably caught my attention, revealing an arrow of smooth yellow skin that directed my gaze to her small, round breasts and sent my imagination roaming downward across her flat abdomen, to the point at which her thighs and torso joined. Her complexion, tawny, flawless, was complemented by only a touch of deep purple lipstick, which enhanced a wonderfully sensuous mouth, firm, full lips parting to reveal regular white teeth, their perfection marred only by a gap between the upper front teeth, a sure sign, local folklore had it, of sexual desire. I prayed the folklore was accurate.

Jesse Florence was the first adult, honest-to-God woman I ever wanted. Each time she entered the store she had my undivided attention. From behind the counter I would watch her every movement, note the slightest change of facial expression, observe each movement of arm and hand, note every contour of her white uniform as it slid over the body I wanted so badly. Trying to be inconspicuous while imagining every detail of the body hidden from my gaze by that crisp white cloth, I would avert my eyes to avoid direct contact with hers, fearful that she might see in them something of what I felt.

While Jesse Florence remained in the store I was so thrilled and embarrassed that I had little time for sexual fantasies. It was impossible both to fantasize and to devote my attention to her, and I much preferred concentrating on the reality of her presence. She must have guessed how I felt about her; I was certainly not the first adolescent to be dazzled by her sensuality. Yet by neither word nor action did she ever indicate the slightest awareness of her effect on me. She always spoke to me pleasantly, and never seemed to view me as anything other than the young white grocery clerk I was, someone who fetched the items she requested, totaled their price, and bagged them.

Once she left, trailing the pungently sweet fragrance of her perfume, my awestruck imagination would recover. Jesse Florence would seduce me repeatedly, for even in my fantasies she was my sexual superior, always the aggressor, too formidable a sexual being for me to hope to conquer. Dreams of sexual conquest were reserved for younger, less imposing quarry, black or white.

Like most boys my age, I was blessed—or cursed—with an active and wildly creative sexual imagination, one which the entrance of teenage black female customers immediately activated. Each girl triggered a specific set of fantasies, usually determined by her particular physical attributes, though sometimes influenced by her personality. Slow business days afforded me ample time to devote to the creation of truly great fantasies. On such days the visit of one girl could generate several elaborately detailed dreams of conquest; a visit by two or three would provoke a veritable orgy of sexual fantasy, although my creativity was inhibited by both my limited experience and my lack of exposure to the fantasies of others, as I lived in a pre-Hefnerian world.

A girl named Charlene frequently played the lead role in some of my better fantasy productions. She wasn't a pretty girl. Except for her eyes, which seemed too small for her great round face, her facial features were much too large. She was a bit overweight, with long skinny legs supporting a thick body to which were attached awkwardly long, thin arms. Charlene was the color of yellowed ivory, perhaps a shade darker. She wore her hair in braids, about shoulder length, a style I didn't find particularly attractive on her. During the winter months Charlene wasn't much to look at, merely another tall, gangly kid wrapped in layers of sweaters and jackets, her form below the waist stuffed into nondescript jeans. But come spring, Charlene underwent a metamorphosis.

No girl in the village could compete with Charlene's bosom measurement. She knew perfectly well what males considered her best attributes and made no effort to hide them. On summer days Charlene would appear dressed in skin-tight shorts and an upper garment revealing the maximum cleavage. Among her favorite garments was a thin blouse, at least three buttons left unfastened, the bottom tied into a knot just above her navel, and worn over a simple bra that struggled to contain her. Another was the strapless elastic halter so popular in the mid-fifties, which, when stretched to its utmost, revealed plenty of Charlene.

Charlene would bounce into the store, sometimes alone, sometimes with a friend or a cluster of girls. She would stroll over to the candy counter, bend forward, placing her hands on her knees, thus assuring that her ample breasts were in full view to anyone on the other side of the glass-encased display case. In this position Charlene would survey our selection of penny candy while I, ogling her breasts through the display case, attempted to move my hands to the candy she selected without diverting my gaze. Fully aware of what held my attention, Charlene enjoyed every moment of my awkwardness, transforming her purchase into a major production often involving any companion who happened to accompany her.

"Let me see now, I believe I'll take two of them Mary Janes," she would announce, bending forward even more, her body swaying up and down ever so slightly, just enough to keep her breasts moving. Occasionally she would bend forward enough to expose a nipple, causing me to forget the selection she had just made.

"What did you say you wanted?" I would ask.

"I say some Mary Janes."

I would reach into the case for the candy, trying not to appear flustered.

"What you think I ought to get, Odel?" she would ask a friend with a giggle, still swaying, as I followed each movement.

"Yeah, give me two packs of Kits and a B-B-Bat."

I would select the requested candy and move to the cash register. Charlene would hand me a nickel, take her candy, and leave, giggling and talking with Odel or Irene or Glenda. I would devote the next few minutes to a flurry of sexual fantasies, all devoted to the erotic dimensions of the upper female form.

Martha Jane, who was three years older than I, also figured prominently in my fantasies. Practically any day of the year, except for the few bitter cold days of winter, I could sit outside, chair leaned back against the sill of a storefront window, and watch Martha Jane hang out clothes, sweep the porch, or talk with friends. She was a slender girl, the color of dark chocolate, well proportioned, with delicate facial features and pointed breasts. My fantasies involving Martha Jane were straightforward and uncomplicated—I imagined getting her in bed, under practically any circumstances. My daydreams about Martha Jane became more urgently physical when, soon after completing high school and still unmarried, she bore a child. Although neither blacks nor whites approved of such events, Martha Jane's family rallied behind her, and she kept the child and remained at home. My reaction to Martha Jane's newly acquired status of motherhood, however, was entirely positive. I saw the child as incontrovertible proof that she had been sleeping with someone and spent hours, without success, trying to determine who. Since she was or certainly had been sleeping with someone, I reasoned, my chances of getting her into bed should have improved. I never mustered the courage to test the validity of my logic, preferring the safety of my fantasies.

Visits to the store by Glenda and Odel invariably brightened my day. A couple of years younger than I, Glenda began to be noticed by the village boys, black and white, at about the time she turned thirteen. She was a strikingly pretty girl, and knew it. A well-developed, beautifully shaped body did nothing to diminish her confidence. She was spoiled, the only girl and the youngest child in a family with four boys. Among the black kids, Glenda had the reputation for being sassy, which meant that she occasionally said what she thought to whites or failed to address them with the traditional "sir" or "ma'am." She often came to the store with Odel, a huge girl nearly six feet tall whose black skin, broad nose, and tightly curled hair contrasted with Glenda's light brown skin, soft black hair, and Caucasian facial features.

Despite their strikingly different physical appearances, both girls drew a chorus of approval when passing groups of boys. I occasionally observed them approach across the store's gravel parking area, their every move appreciated by any of the black boys who happened to be about, and by me. When they were together, Odel attracted the more graphic sexual comments or propositions. Alone, Odel seemed incapable of passing a group of young males without provoking exclamations of appreciation for her body, most of which I felt were richly deserved and without exaggeration. She relished the attention, putting more swing into her walk, shouting pointed rejections of the boys' overtures.

"You the one that better look good, boy, 'cause that's all you gonna do, is look," she would reply to the less graphic compliments. Explicit overtures she would answer with a direct challenge to their issuer's manhood.

"Oh, yeah, Curtis Lee? I just might, 'cept you wouldn't know what to do with it if you got it."

Glenda, on the other hand, ignored completely her young male admirers, walking serenely past them without a word, her head tossed back, a disdainful and tantalizingly sexy pout on her face. The girls' individual responses to male advances, and their unique forms, shaped my fantasies about them. About Odel I had quantitative fantasies (number of times, different positions, length of sessions), while fantasies featuring Glenda were devoted to the quality of the experience.

From my perspective, the sad reality was that my sexual contact with Wade's black girls was entirely limited to the realm of fantasy. No matter how I yearned to advance a serious proposition, make a suggestive remark, to squeeze a breast or pinch a thigh, skills I learned and practiced at an appropriate age with white girls, to do so with black girls was out of the question. I could look, but never touch; dream, but take no action to make the dream come true. Black girls remained off limits, forever beyond my reach because I accepted the racial system that placed them there. To be honest, it wasn't a situation I much regretted. The fantasies the girls provoked were enjoyable, and they placed no pressures on me because I didn't have to worry about how black girls would react to actual advances. And at the time, that concern about white girls was problem enough.

Of all the black girls whose physical charms I appreciated, only one caused me to wish that things might be different. Her name was Betty Jo McAllister. She was Jesse Florence's younger sister and exactly my age. We went through the grades together, she in one school, I in another. We knew each other's families. Her father, Luddy, drove a truck for a Fayetteville motor freight company. He was a loquacious, friendly man who loved his family, whiskey, and baseball, in roughly that order. Roy Campanella, the great Dodger catcher, was his favorite player, and Luddy loved to argue Campanella's merits as opposed to those of Yogi Berra of the Yankees, whose side I took. Sometimes, if he had had a drink or two, Luddy would compare Betty Jo's and my progress in school—the courses we were taking, grades received, extracurricular activities engaged in—seemingly taking real pride in the progress of both of us. Betty Jo's mother, Mazzie, remained at home and cared for her and Irene, the youngest of the three girls in the family. Mazzie was a stocky woman, light-skinned like Luddy but not half as sociable. When Mazzie came to the store there was no small talk. She gave her order, paid her money, took her purchases, and left.

Perhaps because she was not yet a woman, Betty Jo lacked the sheer sensuality of Jesse Florence, but she was prettier. She was taller than her older sister and as well proportioned. Like Jesse Florence, she had small, round breasts, and her skin was light enough to tan noticeably in the summer. She wore her thick wavy hair shoulder-length; her high cheek bones emphasized deep-set dark brown eyes. The sexiest thing about Betty Jo was her voice, deep and throaty, each tone charged with an unpretentious, earthy femininity. I could have listened to Betty Joe talk forever. She was the one girl I hoped would come to the store each day, and usually she did.

I wanted Betty Jo, but I didn't fantasize about her much. With Martha Jane or Odel in the store, I worried about whether they noticed the bulge in the front of my jeans. When Betty Jo came to the store alone, I worried about what to say to her. I desperately wanted to find the words that would allow me to learn more of her world, which mirrored mine yet was so far removed from it. The chasm created by race and class and sex, however, was much too

wide to bridge with words, and I rarely managed more than a formal "Can I help you?" If I felt brave I would ask about Luddy or
some other member of the family. If struck by a fit of recklessness I
questioned her about her schoolwork or the won-lost record of the
basketball team at her segregated high school, another consolidated school occupying a campus not two miles from the school I
attended. Her responses were always as brief and tentative as my
questions. While she replied, I was constantly wondering what she
really thought of me, or if she thought of me as a person rather than
as the white boy clerk in my grandfather's store.

During the six years that I worked in the store, years that spanned
the seventh through the twelfth grades for Betty Jo and me, years in
which we watched one another grow toward adulthood, only once
did I really talk with her, establish some contact on a basic human
level. That one conversation occurred just after Luddy died, in our
senior year. Luddy died of a heart attack one weekend that fall while
hunting in the woods about a mile behind his home. His family was
unaware that he had gone hunting and had no idea why he was
missing or where he had gone. So they waited through the weekend,
praying that Luddy was drunk somewhere, afraid to think of him
sober, for they knew that God watched out for fools and drunks but
that the world could be a dangerous place for sober black men.

Several days after the funeral Betty Jo came to the store. I wanted
to say something meaningful to her, a sentence or phrase that would
convey both my sense of loss at Luddy's death and my concern for
her, for the vivacious, sexy, nice seventeen-year-old girl that she
was. Instead I asked if I could help her and took her grocery order. It
was small; I collected the items, totaled their cost and charged them
to Luddy's account. Looking down at the paper bag into which I was
stuffing her purchases, I mumbled that I was sorry about Luddy. She
didn't respond.

"How's your mother?" I asked, again trying to make contact.

She pulled the bag of groceries across the counter but didn't pick
them up. "She's fine," she said, as if to no one, and certainly not to
me.

Then she looked up, as if she had just come in. "She's really fine," she said in a flat, matter-of-fact tone. Then, abruptly, her voice lowered; her husky, throaty tone indicated that I was her audience. "We knew he was dead the night before they found him. We knew for certain."

She paused, but I knew that she intended to tell me how they knew whether I asked or not, so I didn't ask. I just watched Betty Jo's face.

"Me and Mama and Irene been alone for two nights, didn't know where Daddy was. Mama, she called the company first to see if he'd been sent on an out-of-town run. The company, they didn't know where he was. So then, she called the sheriff. Deputy came the next day. They didn't know nothin' neither. Mama, she say not to worry, say Daddy gonna be alright, that he'd be back soon. She say that for two days."

Betty Jo's face remained motionless as she talked, no smile, no light in her eyes, not the slightest expression of sadness or grief. She looked straight toward me, and at me, and continued in hushed tones, her voice so low that I leaned forward to hear her.

"That last night, Mama changed. She didn't say nothin', just sat looking out the window at the dark. Then, about bedtime, we heard him. A hoot owl, he be perched up in that big ole oak tree in the backyard. He start to hooting, over and over, perched up there in that tree, and he don't stop. Mama, she jump up, run outside, chased that owl away. When she come back in, she be crying. She say Daddy was dead; the hoot owl done told her. The next day they found him."

As she ended her story she picked up the bag of groceries. I stood there, at once feeling sorry for her and fascinated by her tale. I wanted to reach out and touch her, to somehow convey what I felt, to at least respond in some meaningful way. But again I fell back on "I'm sorry." Only the added "Betty Jo" expressed a note of personal concern, something more than the expected customary condolences.

Betty Jo never mentioned Luddy's death again, and I never found a way to talk with her on more than a superficial level. One day as graduation approached I asked her if she planned to attend college. She probably considered that a stupid question since her father was dead and the family had no money, but she just said no. My plans for college were complete; I would work at the store during the summer in return for a year's tuition and expenses. I saw her almost every day that summer. After graduation, we lost even the common experience of school to talk about. Separated by race and class and sex, our worlds never touched again, not even at the periphery of their respective spheres. Still, Betty Jo had taught me that she was really no different from the white girls I dated. I wanted her physically, but there were other things about her that I appreciated, and I wanted her to know that. The white society's restrictions on my ability to convey to her what I felt made clearer to me the sinister reality that underlay the deprecating remarks white males directed at black women. Somehow, Betty Jo seemed above all that.

At the time I was not aware of the larger significance of my relationship with Betty Jo, or of the influence she would have on my racial attitudes as an adult. I only knew that I liked her, genuinely appreciated her for what she was as an individual, and not just because she was sexually attractive, although she certainly was that. I hadn't actually given much thought to why Betty Jo was so special, and wouldn't until reality threatened to disturb my fantasies about black girls.

One summer night after graduation I was alone in the store, working late, preparing to close. I had swept the floor, loaded the soft drink box, washed the meat counter, and generally cleaned for the next business day. I was about to lock the doors—it was perhaps 10:30—when Shorty came in.

Shorty was about five or six years older than I. He lived with his father, Randolph, who worked at the sawmill. Shorty left school at sixteen and picked up odd jobs as a day laborer on nearby farms until he joined the army for a two-year hitch. His tour completed, Shorty rejected military life and returned home with no money, no education, and no future. He again entered the pool of young blacks who performed odd jobs and agricultural labor for Wade's farmers. He was, as his nickname implied, short, not over five-five. Shorty considered himself something of a dandy, and when not dressed in his denim work clothes, he loved to dress for an evening out. He favored long sport jackets that reached practically to his knees, making him appear even shorter. He liked bright colors, but paid little attention to color schemes. That night he wore a kelly green jacket that swallowed him; the sleeves extended to the base of his fingers and the square padded shoulders combined with his black pegged pants gave him the appearance of an inverted pyramid. A white-on-white striped shirt and pastel yellow tie completed his outfit. He resembled a caricature of Sammy Davis, Jr., dressed for his role as Sporting Life in "Porgy and Bess."

Shorty had lived a lean, tough life, yet his experiences had not made him a hard person. His pockmarked face, broad nose, and cavernous mouth, however, made him appear tough, an appearance accentuated by his taste in clothing. In fact, Shorty presented the perfect visual stereotype of the vicious black male implanted in the white mentality by generations of racist propaganda. Actually, he was one of the friendliest, most personable young black men in the village, a hustler and a survivor who would talk to anyone and enjoyed the attention his talkativeness sometimes brought him. He especially enjoyed assuming the role of expert, the man with inside information.

As he entered the store that night, Shorty strolled nonchalantly over to the counter.

"Hey, man," he greeted me, leaning forward to place both hands on the counter top. "Looks like you trying to get out of this place."

"Yeah, Shorty, I'm about ready to go," I replied.

"You got time to get me a Coke?" he asked jokingly.

I flipped up the lid on the red drink box and fished out a bottle.

"You're in luck. Put some cold ones on top. Want it opened?" I asked.

"Yeah, and give me a pack of them salted peanuts."

I leaned across the drink box to reach a shelf filled with large glass containers that held peanuts and a variety of crackers locally known as nabs. Removing the lid, I selected Shorty his package of nuts.

"There you go," I said, placing the Coke and nuts on the counter. "That will be sixteen cents, including the tax."

Shorty placed the exact change on the counter top and walked over and sat in one of the wooden chairs on the other side of the store, seemingly unconcerned by my desire to close shop. I came from behind the counter and moved past him to reach a large switch panel on the far wall and flipped the switches for the gas pumps and outside lights to the off position. Shorty, meanwhile, opened his package of peanuts and poured the contents into his Coke, continuing to show no signs of leaving. I decided to see what was on his mind, but first I bolted the doors to prevent any more unwanted customers and took a seat across from him in Granddaddy's favorite chair.

Shorty began his usual chatter, talking first about the heat in the tobacco fields, then about army life, and on to the Dodgers' latest home stand. Then, for reasons I never fully understood, Shorty suddenly stopped his amiable chatter, looked directly at me, and in a flat, dead serious voice asked, "Hey, man, you want some nigger pussy?"

His question caught me completely off guard. I knew at once that this was no joke, no idle conversation. Shorty was not asking a question, he was making an offer. And I knew that he had good reasons for making it, probably financial. What I didn't know, had not the slightest hint about, was who he had in mind. Was it Odel? Charlene? Martha Jane? His sister Lauraetta, a year younger than I and a female version of Shorty? Some "nigger whore" I didn't know? A black woman in the village I did? These thoughts flashed through my mind while I groped for a response that would preserve my dignity as a white male. I realized that I didn't want Shorty to deliver an Odel or a Charlene, and I certainly wasn't interested in a professional. Then I thought of Betty Jo. I couldn't believe it would be Betty Jo, but if it were, I would have been interested. I couldn't explain to Shorty that Betty Jo was the only black girl that I wanted, but if he could deliver her I wouldn't want her because part of her uniqueness was my belief that she was not deliverable. So I lied.

"No, thank you, Shorty. And if I do, I'll get it myself." The unvarnished bravado of my response startled me.

Shorty cocked his head back and threw up his hands, indicating that he knew I was lying on both counts. Aware that his question had surprised me and challenged my notion of manhood, he laughed in an effort to defuse the situation.

"Hey, man, I didn't mean to get you riled. You don't want any, you don't want any."

He picked up his Coke and moved to the door, turned and smiled.

"Maybe some other time, right?"

This parting comment he delivered as a statement of fact rather than a question.

"Yeah, sure, Shorty," I said, regaining my composure. I unlocked the door, and he stepped outside.

I bolted the door behind Shorty and moved over to peer out a storefront window. I stood and watched him walk down the road until he disappeared, blending into the blackness of the night, and wondered who he had in mind. Moving from the window, I cut out the interior lights and left for home through the back door. Still, Shorty's proposition stayed with me, as did my response. I knew I had lied. I wanted Betty Jo. But, I told myself, he couldn't have meant Betty Jo and I knew I was right. That night I slept little. Instead I lay in bed and thought of Betty Jo, and what it would be like to make love to her.

Sam

The segregated South was steeped in guilt, for whites fully understood the moral implications of the fundamental inequity in their society. Most, however, attempted to avoid guilt by deluding themselves. They pretended, and some actually believed, that racism and segregation were not merely acceptable explanations of their region's social order, but a part of the natural, immutable order of things. White children of the South encountered the shopworn defenses of segregation at an early age, and so did I. In Wade, the wise (or those considered wise), the old, the prosperous, the community leaders, all parroted centuries-old dogma that attributed the origins of segregation to a wrathful evangelical Protestant God. "If God had intended for niggers and whites to mix, he would have made them all the same color" was a statement I frequently heard, especially after the Supreme Court in the 1954 *Brown* case overturned the separate-but-equal doctrine under which segregation had flourished. Wade's adults expected me and other youths to accept such statements without dispute, and we usually did. Public disagreement with one's elders was rarely tolerated. Besides, at the time I was having great difficulty determining God's will in practically every area in life and was too confused to debate the issue.

The better educated also employed their version of history to support segregation. A historical defense was favored by Daddy, who had heard it often, and by Ma Ma, who had actually read widely in history, which, next to religion, was her favorite subject.

Most of it, of course, was written by historians who completely
agreed with Kipling's concept of the white man's burden and the
views of former Confederates about slavery and the Civil War.

"Look at Africa," Ma Ma would say if for some reason moved to
defend the southern way of life. "There has never been an African
nation that created a great civilization. It's a land of savages. That's
partly because they're heathen, I guess, living outside God's bless-
ing. What little they have learned they were taught by whites—the
English and the missionaries."

At the store white farmers and workers offered a slightly less
sophisticated version of Ma Ma's argument.

"You ain't never seen a nigger quarterback, now have you boy?"
was a question I was asked more than once. Of course, I always
replied that I had not. It was a truthful reply. In fact, except on
television, I had never seen any quarterback—collegiate or professional.

According to those whites who expressed themselves on the
issue, and most did, nothing could change the status of blacks.
Their inferiority, all whites agreed, had been decreed by nature.
Quite simply, blacks were intellectually incapable of conducting
themselves according to white standards.

"You can educate a nigger all you want, boy," I was often reminded, "but he's still just a nigger. Ain't nothing you do ever gonna
change that."

Basically I accepted segregation. Yet the arguments I kept hearing
Granddaddy's friends advance against the latest challenge to the
system always seemed to ring a bit hollow. I heard nothing that was
totally convincing, no justification that could completely remove nag-
ging doubts. I recognized the problem and knew why the doubts
remained, despite constant reinforcement of segregationist principles. The justifications of segregation I heard repeatedly simply did
not conform to my personal experiences with blacks.

There was no way around this central dilemma. The more I came
to know blacks as individuals, real people with obvious strengths
and weaknesses, with the same emotions and hopes as everyone

else, the more I began to question segregationist logic. What I felt
for and about these people as fellow humans, people I encountered
in a growing variety of situations, increasingly contradicted the
clichés of the segregationist creed. That contradiction generated
my guilt over segregation, a guilt I shared with other whites.

Perhaps I felt more keenly than most whites the guilt produced
by the clash of segregationist doctrine and practice and the readily
perceived human dignity of individual blacks. I doubt it. Since my
awareness of the conflict arose from contact with blacks, it seems
reasonable to assume that most white southerners who had similar
contacts, and many did, experienced the same emotional reactions,
the same doubts. Some, perhaps most, suppressed their feelings,
but it is hard for me to believe that they never experienced them.

The front seat of an automobile was for me one of the most
consistent and troublesome reminders of the ugly realities of segregation. Racial custom required that adult blacks of the opposite
sex occupy the back seat of an automobile driven by an adult white.
Adults of the same sex and different race could, under certain circumstances, occupy the same seat, although males were much
more likely to do so. I encountered the ethical dilemma of the front
seat at about age fourteen. By that time, despite my lack of a driver's license, I was allowed to deliver groceries, ferry customers to
and from the store, even occasionally fetch maids or day laborers.
Granddaddy granted me the privilege because many of Wade's
blacks lacked their own means of transportation and he had better
things to do. It was an opportunity I welcomed, since it bolstered
my ego, placed me behind a steering wheel, and, once rid of the
customer, allowed me to play with the automobile, completely free
of adult interference.

Although I loved driving the car, I quickly came to detest the
ritual of determining who sat where, and because I was not an
adult, the etiquette of segregation was not precise. Black men or
boys presented no problem; they always sat in front with me. Black
women were another matter entirely. I felt ridiculous when forty-
and fifty-year-old women automatically climbed into the back seat.

It embarrassed me, and at first I asked them to sit up front. I felt like a chauffeur with them in the back. Most women responded to my invitation with a polite "No, thank you, son, the back's just fine." My offer, extended because I felt uncomfortable, made them equally uncomfortable.

On the other hand, several black women, most about Mother's age and with close ties to our family, always sat up front. They never bothered to consult me about where to sit; they simply opened the front door and climbed in. Eva Butler, who lived with her three children behind the store, was typical of these women. The daughter of Miss Carrie, a retired schoolteacher who lived with her husband, Jerry McLean, Eva resided next door to her mother. Jerry had known Granddaddy since his days on the farm in the Swamp, and Miss Carrie had known him almost as long. A dark-skinned woman with strong facial features, Eva worked as a domestic for one of Wade's more affluent families. She had an outgoing personality and an air of self-confidence. Eva delighted in teasing me, especially about girls.

"I hear you been courtin' that Williams girl," she might begin a conversation before placing her grocery order. Or, "Who you seeing this weekend? Got some pretty girl lined up, have you?" Or she might taunt me about my sometimes ill-concealed lack of enthusiasm about my work. "Get up, boy," she would say if she caught me reading. "Put down that book and get my groceries. You be the laziest boy I know, that's for sure, just like your Granddaddy say."

I wouldn't have dared tell Eva to sit in the back seat. Had I done so, I undoubtedly would have had my ears pinned back by a retort such as "Who you think you are, boy? A full growed man?" or "Don't you go trying to act above yourself, boy. Just you drive this car and don't worry yourself none about where I be sittin'."

Eva and a few others obviously considered me an adolescent with whom they could, within certain constraints, speak as they chose. I felt more comfortable with them, as if I related to them more as equals. Deferential behavior on the part of blacks, I had discovered, made me feel ill at ease, for what reason I did not yet understand. Older women bothered me most, women like Aunt

Nancy, who must have been in her late sixties. She, too, I occasionally drove home with a load of groceries or picked up for a day of domestic work at our house. Aunt Nancy invariably sat in the back seat, and I would never have asked her to sit up front. Somehow I knew that she belonged to another generation and would refuse if asked. And so, over a period of about a year, I gradually learned which black women I could expect to sit in the back, which would sit up front, and which I could ask to sit up front without making everyone concerned feel uncomfortable. Black girls, of course, were not a problem. Here the rule was simple. Never, under any circumstances, would I have been alone with them in an automobile.

The stark poverty endured by many of Wade's blacks also disturbed me. I found it increasingly difficult to accept and impossible to justify. Wade had its poor whites, but none who lived at the level of poverty to which several black families at the bottom of the village's economic ladder were accustomed. Their poverty, which I saw daily, fed my growing sense of racial guilt. So, too, did some of my reactions to it.

Among Wade's poorest blacks were the families of the loggers, the men who felled the towering pines upon which much of the local economy depended. Tart's sawmill did not employ them directly, for such an arrangement would have afforded them the protection of federal labor law, federal minimum wages, and social security benefits. Of course, at the time I didn't understand this. I knew only that the loggers were hired by "woods bosses," so-called "independent contractors" who furnished timber to the sawmill. Many of the woods bosses were black. Each worked a crew of from ten to twenty men. The boss supplied the tools and equipment—chain saws, log skidders, trucks—required to fell and trim the trees and transport the logs to the mill. Since the logs were cut and sold entirely within the state, and the workers technically were employed by the bosses, not the mill, they were exempt from federal labor laws. The loggers received no retirement benefits, no social security, no workmen's compensation. They were covered only by the state minimum wage, which went from sixty to seventy-five cents

per hour while I lived in Wade. Inclement weather cut into their
work time, and some bosses deducted charges for "supplies" from
their wages. Their work was difficult, dirty and dangerous, but
many preferred it to the seasonal agricultural day labor which was
their only alternative.

The family of a particular logger, Bruce Carter, forced me to
comprehend the meaning of the poverty many blacks faced daily. It
was not a lesson for which I was grateful. There was no sudden
revelation brought about by some single emotional experience,
such as that with Bobo. Rather, it was a lesson learned gradually,
drawn from hundreds of encounters with Bruce and his children.

Bruce was a slender, withered, yellow-skinned man in his late
fifties. He had spent his life in the log woods, and accidents and
strenuous labor had left him stooped and drained. I remember the
stumps of fingers on his left hand, graphic evidence of the dangers
of his work. Bruce had a house full of children, whom I assumed
were cared for by his wife, one of the few blacks in Wade I rarely
encountered. She never came to the store; it was Bruce or one of
his children I saw. The older boys worked as farm laborers to sup-
plement the family income, and the younger children ran errands
for the family.

Three of the Carter children I will never forget. One was the
oldest boy, three or four years my senior, whose real name I never
knew. He was called Skunky by the older black kids because his
personal hygiene could have been greatly improved. Skunky had
dropped out of school in the seventh or eighth grade and was practically illiterate. It was painful to watch him laboriously endorse an
occasional check received in payment for day labor. Too young to
be recruited for the logging crews, Skunky worked for several area
farmers during the summer and fall, usually in tobacco fields. He
came into the store on Friday evenings with a week's wages and
purchased a pair of jeans or a new work shirt, and perhaps a few
staples to take home for the family. Later in the weekend I might
see him dressed in his latest Friday purchase, already caught up in
the cycle of a hard week's work and a drunken weekend, which
depleted his limited bank roll.

Skunky came into the store, and I waited on him. He stated, directly and simply, what he wanted, and I got it for him, bagged it, and collected his money. Skunky, for obvious reasons, was not extended credit. We never talked; there were no exchanges about baseball and boxing, no talk of cars, movies, or any other racially "safe" topic. Skunky was isolated by his poverty even from most of Wade's blacks, and I held him in contempt. And yet, as time passed, I came to recognize the tragedy he represented, to see him as victim. I both loathed and pitied him. The summer I left Wade, nothing had changed. Skunky was still there, working the tobacco fields, spending on weekends what he earned that week, living one day to the next.

Skunky's two youngest siblings were a boy who, when I was fifteen, was about five or six, and a sister a year younger. I never knew their names either. They often came to the store to purchase some item that was needed immediately. Sometimes, before presenting themselves to be waited on, they would stand and stare longingly at the contents of the candy counter. Summer or winter, their clothes were in tatters; they appeared unkempt, even filthy. They always seemed to be afflicted by some painfully obvious ailment—a runny nose, the red swelling of sore eyes, festered cuts, and scrapes left unattended. I doubt that they ever saw either a doctor or a dentist, for Wade had no public health personnel, and the Carters had no way of traveling to the county clinic in Fayetteville.

I responded with anger to the undeniable reality of their extreme poverty. It was an affront to my world of position and plenty, one I preferred not to acknowledge. They would come into the store on a winter's day, carrying a clear glass gallon jug, its mouth closed with a corn cob stopper, to buy kerosene for the space heater that warmed their home. If Granddaddy or Mother was in the store, I would ignore the children, hoping to avoid acknowledging what I regarded as their pathetic existence.

"Get up, boy, see what those kids want," Granddaddy would order.

"What you want?" I would ask, almost threateningly, hating them because they were black and poor, because their very presence gave the lie to the segregationist cant about contented blacks, because they made me uncomfortable.

"Mama say she want a gallon of coal oil," the boy would reply.

"Let me have the jug." I would come from behind the counter, take the jug, go outside and fill it at the hand-operated kerosene pump, and return.

"That's twenty cents. You got any money?"

"Mama say tell you to charge it."

I would watch them leave, the boy's body bent downward by the weight of the kerosene-filled jug, the girl tagging along behind him. On other days they wrestled with ten-pound bags of potatoes, or a gallon of milk, or a bag of canned goods. It never occurred to me to offer them a ride home. They were so poor as to be undeserving. I would stand and watch them walk off toward home, and hope the ground would open and swallow them up. The connection between their poverty and their race was all too obvious. Their presence was an indictment of segregation, an inescapable accusation of my complicity in it. From the age of fifteen or so, I never saw Bruce's two youngest children without feeling a twinge of guilt and without hating them for what I felt. To ease that guilt, sometimes I did as generations of whites had done: I was "good to" Bruce's kids.

"Here," I would say, reaching into the candy counter, "want some candy?" After two affirmative nods of the head, I would pull out two pieces of penny candy, Mary Janes or Bits of Honey.

"There you go," I would hold out the candy to them. The two would reach up, take the candy, and leave without a word. There was no "thank you," no "you're welcome." Even at our ages, we understood that my giving was a ritual, not an act of generosity. It was a ritual I repeated many times.

It was not just poor blacks like Bruce Carter's family who made me feel uneasy about segregation, however. After a few years at the store, I understood that even the most prosperous of Wade's blacks were deemed inferior. Ed Smith taught me that lesson, or rather the treatment he received did. Again, no single traumatic incident involving Ed enlightened me about the pervasive impact of segregation. Rather, it was a series of nonevents, little slights, casual remarks, that led to my awareness.

Ed was my grandfather's age, one of Wade's few black land-owners. Through a combination of hard work, meticulous attention to the details of farming, and the constant frugality of the ambitious poor, he and his family had coaxed a good living from his small farm. He and his wife, Lilly, a large, soft-spoken woman, had brought up a large family, three boys and two girls. Ed and Lilly had sent through college all the children who wanted to go. Three of them, one of the boys and both of the girls, left the South. The youngest boy became a teacher; Ed's middle son obtained a civil service position at Fort Bragg. Within the black community they were a family of substance, better off economically, and better educated, than many of Wade's whites.

Ed himself was a short, compact man, slow of movement and speech, naturally taciturn, and possessed of a keen, dry wit. A gray fringe encircled his bald forehead, lending him a dignified appearance, enhanced by the pipe he always carried. Ed was well mannered and well spoken, always careful to use standard English, precisely pronounced. He was honest and hardworking, qualities that white southerners professed to respect. His family, and his wife's family, had lived in Wade for generations.

Ed's achievements did not go totally unnoticed or unrewarded by the white community. More than any other black, Ed commanded the respect of Wade's "best whites." I saw my grandfather and father talk at length with Ed about the condition of crops, the health of village residents, even Wade's need for improvements such as paved streets and services such as medical care.

Such conversations, however, involved only Ed and either Daddy or Granddaddy, and certain topics of white men's conversation, especially women and politics, were never mentioned. Ed lived no more than five hundred yards behind the store, and he came in often, especially in late afternoon or on rainy days. Yet he was never admitted into the circle of Granddaddy's friends who gathered at the

store each night and many afternoons. On a few occasions he would
sit just outside the circle, balanced on an upturned soda crate, and
listen, but he never joined the conversation unless directly addressed, a rare occurrence. That he sat on the outside looking in led
me to believe that Ed wanted to be included, that he felt he could
acquit himself well in the conversational jousting that was both an
integral part of the social life of the community and a traditional
means of proving one's worth. I imagined that he always hoped, at
some magic moment in the future, to be asked to join the group, none
of whom, I suspect, he believed to be his superior. I may have been
wrong about Ed, misinterpreted his body language as he stood, foot
rested on a drink crate, elbow on knee, chin in hand, listening on the
outside of the circle. He may not have cared. In any case, he was
never given the opportunity. I came to understand that he never
would be admitted, no matter how much he deserved to be. It wasn't
fair and I knew it, and I found that knowledge troublesome. Ed's
exclusion, however, was not something I dwelt upon at the time, and
it in no way altered my behavior toward him. When I was fifteen and
he was nearly seventy, I still called him Ed. There were no black
"misters" in Wade.

My racial guilt was not solely the by-product of injustices observed. As one of Wade's "best whites" I was expected never to
"behave badly" toward blacks. For friends less constrained by social imperatives, however, taunting blacks was a favored and totally
acceptable pastime. While not encouraging the sport, the boys' parents seldom objected to it. I occasionally joined in their activities,
though I never participated in actions designed to inflict pain or
bodily injury. At least that is what I prefer to believe. Perhaps I
lacked the courage (for it required a perverted sort of physical
courage) to engage in my friends' rock wars—to hurl fist-sized
chunks of granite picked from railway beds across the tracks at
unwary black youngsters—or to shoot BB guns at blacks, who
sometimes shot back. And there were other reasons, more immediately physical, for avoiding such overt acts of racism. Even the
less violent racist behavior in which I did engage, had it been dis-

covered by my parents, would have earned me a "tanning"—
Mother's favored weapon being the thin willow switches we were
forced to break ourselves; my father's, his leather belt. Faced with
such unhappy alternatives, I naturally made every effort to keep
secret my breaches of what Mother and Daddy considered proper
racial etiquette. Attempts to conceal such escapades, of course,
only heightened my guilt about participating in them.

I first understood that the memories of these racial episodes
were a permanent part of my mental baggage, and the import of
that fact, when I read Harper Lee's *To Kill a Mockingbird* as a
college freshman. Oddly enough, Tom Robinson, the ultimate victim of racial violence in her novel, stirred no racial memories for
me. I understood the significance of Tom's fate intellectually, because I understood that his predicament was a possibility all black
males confronted. But I had never known a black male actually
accused, like Tom, of raping a white woman, and so the character
elicited no personal response.

Rather, it was the character Boo Radley, or, more accurately, the
initial reaction of the Finch children to his mysterious and threatening presence, that caught my attention. Curious about and afraid of
the reclusive Boo, who was portrayed by town gossips as the local
boogey man, Jim and Scout Finch mustered enough courage to approach and touch the Radley house, all the while expecting a ferocious Boo to reach out of the darkness and drag them off to some
unspeakable fate. Boo Radley triggered memories saturated with
guilt. My Boo Radley had been not an emotionally disturbed white
recluse, but a black man named Sam McNeil.

To me as a youth, Sam was every bit as mysterious and threatening as Boo. When I was about eleven or twelve, Sam had returned to the community after an incarceration of several years in
what whites referred to as "the colored insane asylum." It was
rumored that Sam had killed a man, knocked him to the ground in a
fit of anger and crushed his skull. I believed it, in part because I had
heard Mother and Daddy say he had killed someone, although they
never discussed how. Sam became our boogey man, a menacing

presence in our childhood world. He looked the part. He was a thickset man over six feet tall, who dressed in loose-fitting blue denim overalls that emphasized his considerable girth. We were told to avoid Sam because he "wasn't right," but Sam didn't seem crazy to me—slightly retarded, perhaps, but not crazy. Because of his size and color, adult whites regarded him with fear and suspicion. The man I came to know, however, was genuinely friendly and delighted in any opportunity to please.

Because he seldom came to the store, I saw Sam less often than most of Wade's blacks. He lived with a brother and sister-in-law on the outskirts of the village. Perhaps to avoid the unkind remarks and concerned glances of whites who were curious about him because he was "different," Sam stayed close to home. Because of his great physical strength and his obvious desire to please, however, whites hired him for tasks that required heavy manual labor, and my family was no exception. His sporadic appearances at the house to perform odd jobs (always over Mother's objections: "I just don't like having that man around the house," she'd say) gave me the opportunity to talk with him. I soon came to the conclusion that Sam hardly represented a threat to anyone.

Once he helped Daddy repair a hand pump that stood beneath a magnificent old water oak which grew next to our garden. We used the pump, which was some distance from the house, to obtain water for the garden during summer droughts. After several hours' work in the garden under a hot sun, we would come to the pump, splash water over our heads, and gulp down draughts of ground-cooled water from the mouth of the pump. As Sam labored I pestered him with questions about how the pump worked. He answered me patiently and in great detail, demonstrating how each part of the pump operated to pull the water from the ground. His repairs finished, he tested his work by pumping a glass of water for me. He asked me to pump for him while he washed up, which I did, and then he leaned over to drink from his cupped hands as I continued to work the pump handle.

"This here's good water," he said, obviously pleased with his work. "Clean and cool. Course, you don't want to go drinking too much on a day hot as this."

"Why not?" I asked, my curiosity piqued.

"Well sir," he explained, wiping his face with a large bandanna pulled from a back pocket, "this here water's so cool and clean that if you're too hot and you drink too much, it can kill you. And that's a fact."

Sam paused to glance at me to check the effect of his assertion, realized that I doubted his word, and continued in an effort to convince me.

"You think I be funning you, do you boy?" he began, smiling at the thought. "Well, I ain't. It's the pure truth. It kilt ole man Williams. Not water from this pump, but one just like it, least ways. He been working in the field all morning, come up to the pump all hot and sweaty and drank him a belly full of water. Well, all that cold water stopped his heart—right then and there, kilt him deader'n a doornail."

Sam had me convinced and alarmed. I thought in horror of all the times I had come from the garden, hot and sweaty just like ole man Williams, to drink from our pump.

"You reckon this water can kill me?" I asked, hoping for a negative response.

"Oh, no, boy," he laughed, "don't you worry none about that. You have to be working hard in the sun, sweating hard, for a long time, then drink you a belly full of water."

Sam probably couldn't imagine me working hard in a field all morning, an indication that his perceptions about people were accurate.

"Just you remember, though, when you be real hot, just you drink a little water, 'till you cooled down some." With that advice Sam collected his tools and walked back toward the house where my father waited to drive him home once his task was completed.

After the incident at the pump I decided that I definitely liked Sam. Mother's warning against speaking to Sam because he was "peculiar" and therefore could never be trusted completely now

seemed absurd. Other encounters with Sam did nothing to change
my newly formed opinion of him or my decision to ignore Mother's
advice. From then on, when I saw Sam, I spoke, and he always
returned my greeting. Sam, I noticed, seemed a bit withdrawn,
with a dreamlike quality that I never noticed in other adults. He
responded to questions and comments more slowly than most
grownups, but his response always seemed to me reasonable, and I
never found his behavior threatening in the least. I didn't think of
Sam as a friend, even as I grew older, but I considered him a
harmless and rather likable member of the community. My view of
Sam, however, was shared by neither adult whites nor my young
friends. To them Sam remained an almost subhuman creature, a
thing to be scorned and feared.

Reading about Boo Radley years later would conjure up suppressed memories of a particularly mean race-baiting incident in
which I participated, and of which Sam was the victim. It occurred
when I was twelve or thirteen, on a sultry summer's night. It was
one of those evenings common in July and August, when the op-
pressive heat and humidity of the day lingered into the night, de-
priving people of sleep and setting nerves on edge. Like most kids,
I loved these heat-filled evenings, with their long twilights that
stretched into a warm, lazy darkness. On such evenings most parents, in an effort to escape the combined effects of stultifying heat
and noisy youngsters, sent their children outside. In most homes
supper was finished by seven and the children dismissed soon
thereafter. Younger children were expected to return home as the
long summer day faded into darkness, but boys older than twelve
or so were allowed to remain out until ten, later on weekends.
Parents may perhaps have been concerned about accidental injury:
every now and then a child would cut a foot on broken glass or fall
and break a limb, and there was always the worst possibility, that a
child would be hit by an automobile. There was no fear that village
residents would harm their children, for parents knew every vil-
lager, most of whom were themselves parents or grandparents. We
were free, released from adult supervision, and I reveled in the

long stretches of unstructured time. The village was our play-ground, and the cover of darkness afforded opportunities for games we dared not play during the day.

This particular evening began like most others, with a gathering of boys under sixteen—those who lacked a driver's license or a friend who had that coveted piece of paper. Adolescence among males was divided into pre- and post-automobile stages, and gaining access to the family automobile was our most meaningful rite of passage. Without transportation we younger males were confined to the vil-lage limits. Bicycles expanded our daytime range, but parents frowned upon their use at night because of the increased possibility of a collision with a car. So at night we relied on our feet, walking in packs from one corner of the village to the other, "looking for trou-ble," adults said, though in Wade there was little serious trouble to be found.

The gathering was an important part of the evening ritual. Never organized, it occurred spontaneously, since we each knew where to head once dismissed from the supper table. On this night we met in a small vacant lot behind Howard Lee's house, where we played a modified version of softball. We used a "ball" made of rags stuffed into an old sock, tied at the end, which we whacked with bats whit-tled from rejected one-by-four lumber. Perfect for a restricted space and quicker paced than baseball, the game had the added advantage of safety—a rag ball did little damage when batted onto a pitcher's shin or hurled into a hitter's ear. Our number increased as the game progressed, reaching a dozen or more, and we played until the batters could no longer see the ball in the red twilight cast by a sun already beneath the horizon.

After the game ended, most of the players drifted home. Those of us who stayed retreated to the concrete slabs atop the red brick pillars that flanked the wooden steps leading to Howard's front porch. There we debated the most exciting way to spend what remained of our evening. Except for John Douglas, Howard's younger brother, who was about ten and didn't really count, I was the youngest member of the group. Dennis Hobson, Harold Walker

Jones, and Tommy Lee rounded out the membership. Harold Walker and Dennis were the oldest, both about fifteen, and the natural leaders. Dennis lived with his mother two doors down from the Joneses in a house rented from the mill. His parents were divorced, a rarity in Wade, and Dennis's father came to visit him each summer. The father's appearance I can't recall, but the memory of his shiny black 1952 Buick with its sloping trunk, graceful rear fenders, and elongated hood filled with glittering rows of chrome rings remains fresh. Dennis was a tough kid, wiry and strong, and possessed of a not altogether undeserved reputation as the neighborhood rough-neck. Harold Walker, the son of the community's electrician, lived directly across the street from my grandmother, and he, like Dennis, had an imaginative mean streak.

We talked as the twilight dwindled, reaching no decision until the heavy, tepid darkness, filled with chirps of frogs and crickets and permeated by the lingering smells of just-consumed dinners, enveloped us. We decided to walk to Noah Bullock's store, located across the village near the highway, about ten minutes away. We struck out under Harold Walker's leadership as Howard Lee, in an effort to avoid the embarrassment of a younger brother, sought to convince John Douglas to stay home. Undeterred, John Douglas followed at a respectful distance. After skipping a few rocks at John Douglas, who artfully dodged them all, Howard made the best of the situation and ignored him.

Mr. Noah's store held a special attraction that summer: an ambience of violence and death created by one of the most spectacular murders in village history. Though the murder had occurred months earlier, the excitement of the crime still reverberated through the village. People continued to gather at Mr. Noah's to recall, and no doubt derive some vicarious pleasure from, the thrill of a violent death.

The shooting had occurred late one afternoon, in that brief, leisurely period at dusk between the end of the work day and the evening meal. At this hour the village stores were filled with customers: housewives purchasing extra ingredients for a supper nearly prepared, workers from the mill relaxing with a Coke, a few commuters stopping in on their way home from Fayetteville, since Mr. Noah's store also served as the local bus stop. It was such a crowd that Mary Lou Adams startled, bursting into the store and slamming the screen door shut behind her. Pursuing her was her husband, Martin. A withdrawn, brooding man, he was one of the few blacks whom white residents feared.

Mary Lou's obvious terror silenced the crowd. Instinctively realizing that she was in immediate danger and represented a possible threat to them, the crowd shied away, leaving her alone in the middle of the store. Suddenly a shotgun blast ripped through the screen and struck her in the chest, driving her body backward across the room. She collapsed to the floor, her blood flowing out to stain the worn hardwood boards, creating dark splotches we would gaze at months later. For an instant the onlookers stood stunned, and then moved slowly forward and ringed the body. Meanwhile, Martin ran to his car and sped off down the highway.

News of the shooting spread through the village instantaneously, as if the residents communicated by mental telepathy. Within half an hour an ambulance had arrived from Fayetteville to collect the body, and sheriff's deputies were questioning witnesses. Already crowds had gathered outside the store. Inquisitive mothers combatted the efforts of equally inquisitive youngsters to glimpse the corpse; denim-clad farmers elbowed their way to the inner edge of the crowd for a better view; workers from the city decried violent blacks and whispered rumors that infidelity caused the shooting. The whites gazed at the jagged hole in the screen, while a number of blacks lingered at the crowd's edge, discussing the crime in hushed tones. People milled about until Mr. Noah closed the store, and then the crowd gradually drifted away to spread the news to the uninformed. The police captured Martin the next day. Tried and convicted, he would complete his sentence and return to Wade before I graduated from high school. Many of Wade's whites saw the crime as simply another "nigger shooting," exciting but of no real consequence. That view was obviously shared by the courts.

As we approached Mr. Noah's that night, our minds were filled with macabre thoughts of the murdered Mary Lou. Somewhere in the darkness might lurk a black waiting to fire a shotgun blast into our ranks. We were alert to every night sound, aware of each shrub or tree behind which an assailant might crouch, frightened by the long, flickering shadows cast by the floodlights that illuminated the orange GULF sign towering over our destination. Our paranoia increased as we drew near the store, and we instinctively closed ranks, each hoping that any burst of fire from the night would strike a friend rather than himself. We quickened our pace, anxious to escape the darkness and reach the illuminated storefront area, breaking into a run as we covered the last few yards of unpaved street between us and the safety of the asphalt drive that led to the store. Breathless from fright and the exertion of our sprint out of the dark, we piled upon a wooden bench usually reserved for passengers awaiting a Trailways bus.

Once safely in the reassuring yellow-orange glow of the store's lights, we quickly regained our composure. Our courage also returned with the knowledge that there were adults inside. Up close, the murder scene held none of the mystery and danger we had imagined while walking through the dark, and a quick examination of the screen door, now neatly repaired, left us with little to do. Unwilling to return home and unable to purchase candy or soft drinks because none of us had any money, we sat on the bench and rehashed the murder.

"Who's inside?" someone asked, seeking to alleviate our boredom and probably hoping that the store's customers might entertain us with another shooting.

Reasserting his leadership after our unorganized dash to safety, Harold Walker left the bench to peer through a window in an effort to answer the question. "Nobody much," he said, face pressed to the window, "just Mr. Noah and Mr. Ronald and that crazy nigger Sam."

The mention of Sam's name stopped our chatter and rekindled our fears, and we again envisioned some black assailant awaiting us out there in the night we had just fled.

"I hear he killed somebody, too," Dennis spoke up, doing nothing to relieve our revived apprehensions. "Didn't shoot him, though, killed him barehanded—strangled him to death."

Dennis's account of the incident rattled my recently acquired faith in Sam's peaceable nature.

"He's a mean nigger, all right," Tommy joined in the speculation about Sam. "My daddy says you never can tell what a nigger like that will do. He says he shouldn't be allowed to live in Wade."

"What's he doing in there?" asked Dennis, unable to see around Harold Walker, who refused to yield his position in front of the window.

"He ain't doing nothing, just standing there. What'd you expect him to be doing?" Harold Walker replied sarcastically, as if Dennis would be disappointed that Sam was not threatening to knife someone.

"He don't look so mean to me," Harold added.

"Sure, he don't," Dennis shot back. "That's because he's in there. Besides, I ain't seen you get close to him."

Dennis's challenge appealed to Harold's mean streak. "Well, I bet we could get him good and mad."

"Oh, yeah, how?" Dennis asked, intrigued by the idea and unwilling to appear more frightened of Sam than was Harold Walker.

"Yell something at him, see what he does," replied Harold.

"Like what?"

By now the banter between Harold and Dennis had captured our attention, our adrenaline flowing at the thought of the excitement such a proposal might create.

"How about 'Nigger, Nigger'?" Howard Lee suggested, answering Dennis's question.

We all knew "Nigger, Nigger." It was one of the chants we used in childhood games, a counting chant like "Eeny, Meeny, Miney, Mo, Catch a Nigger by the Toe," but more vicious.

"Yeah, 'Nigger, Nigger,'" the group agreed, knowing that if it failed to enrage Sam, nothing would.

"All right," Harold Walker approved of our suggestion. "I'll open the door and you all yell. Then run like hell."

We nodded in agreement, jumped off the bench and, screwing up our courage, moved to the door. Harold Walker moved up to the front of the pack and swung the door open as we chanted on cue:

Nigger, nigger black as tar
Stuck his head in a molasses jar.
Jar broke, cut his throat,
Went to hell on a billy goat.

We were off and running before the last syllable was uttered, stumbling over one another in a mad flight from the store lights into the darkness we had fled only minutes ago, but which now offered sanctuary from the wrath of a vengeful Sam, whom we imagined bursting through the door in hot pursuit, ranting and raving at his tormentors. I was terrified, running as if my life depended on it and convinced that it did; running with no regard for others or for obstacles that might lay in my path; running with my heart pounding, my mouth open, inhaling great gulps of warm night air. I ran as if in a nightmare in which some hideous monster was bearing down on me, poised to rip my body to shreds, and my feet, no matter how swiftly they moved, could not transport me quickly enough from the danger. We left John Douglas, who ran behind crying, begging us to wait. He was as convinced as we were that Sam would snatch him up to snap him in two or squeeze the life from his body.

We did not stop running until we reached the Presbyterian church, about half a mile down the street. Easily outdistancing the rest of us, Dennis veered across the churchyard and ran up the massive steps that led to the church entrance, probably convinced that not even a deranged and furious Sam would invade the house of God. The rest of us followed him, gasping for air as we staggered up the steps. We collapsed on the hard concrete portico floor and sagged backward to lean against the red brick walls.

I was too scared to talk, but Howard Lee voiced our collective fears. "Did you see him? Is he coming?"

"I didn't see nobody," Harold Walker answered, "but he may be out there."

"Maybe we should go back," Dennis spoke up, emboldened by his successful flight to the church.

"Okay," Harold agreed. "Let's go down to the street and see."

We filed down the steps and walked to the street, where we peered into the darkness toward Mr. Noah's, half expecting to see a monstrous black figure charging down upon us. There was no sign of Sam. The only person in sight was John Douglas, panic-stricken and trying desperately to catch up with the group.

"I guess he ain't coming," Howard said, obviously relieved.

We knew he was right. Sam wasn't coming; in fact, he had probably never left the store. We realized no vengeful madman had chased us, threatening to tear us limb from limb, that we had never been in danger. There was very little additional conversation, because we were each ashamed of our fear, of our wild scramble to the church, of ignoring one another in the face of imagined danger, of abandoning John Douglas. We all went home.

I walked home through the night thinking about Sam, not the ferocious figure of our collective imagination whom we had fled, the deranged monster who threatened us with mutilation, but the Sam who had fixed our pump and cautioned me about drinking too much water on a hot summer's day; the gentle, slightly befuddled Sam I had seen so many times. There was, I knew, no excuse for my behavior, and with that knowledge came a growing sense of guilt. It sprang partly from the realization that I had betrayed the family's expectations, especially Mother's, that I had violated the basic human dignity that my family acknowledged blacks possessed. Yet there was another sense of betrayal, deeper, more personal. I realized that I had hurt Sam, had hurt him deliberately, and, worst of all, had hurt him with the fact of his race. I knew that Sam had done nothing to deserve our actions, and that I had betrayed the kindness he had shown me.

The episode with Sam didn't end that night; it stretched on for years. In all the time I remained in Wade I never saw Sam that I did not recall the details of that night at Mr. Noah's, and remember "Nigger, nigger black as tar." Of course, I never apologized to Sam or admitted my guilt, nor did I ever again mention the incident to anyone, not even those involved. To salve my conscience I tried to be nicer to Sam, to be a bit more polite when we met, to make sure I greeted him with words that conveyed my recognition of his worth as a person. But penance and restitution had no place in the system of segregation, for they threatened white supremacy by calling into question the actions of whites and admitting the basic humanity of blacks. And so the guilt from my episode with Sam remained, as did the guilt from hundreds of lesser racial confrontations, a legacy of my region that I would put into perspective only after years of internal conflict and the emotionally tumultuous years of the civil rights revolution.

Granddaddy and Viny Love

My attitudes about race remain irrevocably linked to memories of Granddaddy, who, more than any other white, helped to form them. He was a complex man, intelligent, proud, aloof, and supremely confident of his own abilities. He was also a profoundly unhappy man, plagued by some deep-seated, unarticulated lack of fulfillment. He battled life without ever coming to terms with it, never achieving peace with himself. The variety of names by which he was known, names I heard every day, revealed the complexity of the man, and much about his nature. To my brothers, sisters, and me, he was Granddaddy. My father always referred to him as "my daddy," as if the two words were one; my mother called him Daddy Mac. Ma Ma, Olivia, and close friends called him Lonnie; friends who were not members of his inner circle referred to him as Lonnie Mac. Blacks called him Mr. Lonnie, at least in his presence; salesmen and casual acquaintances called him Mac. He often jested that his initials, A. A., stood for Alonzo Alphonso, but his real name was Albert (for an uncle) Alonzo (for God knows who) McLaurin. I remember hearing him referred to by either given name only once—at his funeral, by a minister whose name I cannot recall.

Granddaddy, through example, instructed me in the paternalistic nature of segregation. He was like a god to many of Wade's blacks, especially the older ones, or so it seemed to me. They came to him for credit to put groceries on their tables and gasoline in their cars. And if times were really desperate, they came to borrow money— hard cash to get a wife into a hospital, to pay for the delivery of a baby, to prevent the family from being evicted by an unrelenting landlord, to save the automobile from being repossessed by an instant-credit used car dealer, to purchase a bus ticket to send a promising black child "up north." They knew that if he trusted them, if he held them in some esteem, and if he believed they made every effort to pay their debts, Mr. Lonnie would usually come through. By the time I was fourteen, I was familiar with Granddaddy's account ledgers, had seen entry after entry closed with a red line and the words "bad debt." Each of those closed entries, and there were two and three under some names, represented people I knew and often saw. I thought Granddaddy was a soft touch. I doubt many blacks perceived him quite that way.

Some of the older blacks looked to Mr. Lonnie for more than money or credit. They sought his advice on how to cope with a grown son gone bad, or on whether and when they should attempt to buy land, a house, an automobile. Seeking jobs, they asked his aid—some word of recommendation to prospective employers, a magic incantation that would ensure their selection. For many he was their link to "the system," their contact with the modern world, a world that passed them by while they followed a mule-drawn plow through the cool, upturned earth in the middle of a sun-parched field on some godforsaken tenant farm. Mr. Lonnie cashed state and federal checks for the old, the blind, welfare recipients, without charge. At the first of every month they came, checks in hand. If the recipients were illiterate, Granddaddy would forge their names, ignoring the formalities required for such transactions. I would sometimes see him sign a dozen or more checks within the first few days of the month. Everyone knew that Mr. Lonnie would give them exactly the face value of the check. Some never knew the amount of their check, they simply handed it to him and accepted the money he offered, no questions asked.

Other blacks feared him, and some probably hated him. He was The Man. At any moment he could demand payment of debts incurred for the necessities of life, refuse further extensions of credit, deny requests for loans to buy medicine for a sick child or a train ticket to visit a relative. I have seen the whites of eyes, widened by anger, flash on black faces when, after a quarter of an hour of desperate pleading, Granddaddy rendered a negative verdict. If they continued to press their appeal after his response, he dismissed the supplicant without contempt but without empathy, with the steel-hard finality of the one in charge, the boss, The Man. And I have seen grown men, black men twice the size of Granddaddy, choke back their anger and frustration, and in their helplessness turn abruptly and silently stalk out of his store, their hopes and plans dashed by his final and unequivocal no. To some blacks Granddaddy must have seemed a tyrant, a benevolent one perhaps, but a tyrant nonetheless.

He swore like a tyrant. It was one of his best-developed talents, an ability that added immeasurably to his aura of indomitability. He ranked with the most forceful and effective swearers I have ever encountered, in part because he never abused the art. He rarely used strong language in normal conversation, rather, his cursing was always calculated for the greatest effect. His blasts of profanity were withering, yet never vulgar or self-conscious. He avoided sexual and scatological phrases, relying instead on a relatively few favored curses which he employed with skill and precision, carving away the dignity of an individual with the vehemence of his profanity or hurling his oaths so forcefully at inanimate objects that thwarted his will as to cause them almost visible damage. I once heard him curse an uncooperative oil heater with such ferocity that I thought his words alone would demolish it.

Son-of-a-bitch and bastard were his favorites. He could call a man a hundred kinds of a son-of-a-bitch and practically as many kinds of a bastard. I always thought there was a rough fairness, one might even say democracy, about his swearing. He applied his profanity without prejudice to members of both races, rich or poor, powerful or powerless. He would call a black a goddamned dishonest son-of-a-bitch and welching no-account bastard, but on occasion he would denounce whites who failed to meet his expectations with equal fervor. He never called blacks dumb or stupid, never joked about their sexual activities, and never implied that they were less than human, although he clearly held them to be inferior. As a village merchant, he naturally reserved his most effective profanity for debtors who refused to pay, whether they were white or black.

Despite the democratic nature of his profanity, Granddaddy shared all the basic racial prejudices of the society. He could, and did, denounce blacks with a ferocity seldom heard in his characterizations of offending whites. Blacks who failed to pay their debts or to perform some promised service, or who in some way seriously inconvenienced him, were roundly condemned, though rarely to their faces. There were face-to-face encounters, however, usually over his refusal to grant requests for loans or extensions of credit. The few I witnessed became heated only when Granddaddy was convinced that no tactic other than a blast of profanity would persuade his supplicant that he meant no. He also had a habit of comparing behavior of mine that he found objectionable to what he considered characteristically black behavior. Such remarks covered topics as diverse as my attitudes about work, my promptness, or rather my tardiness, and my eating habits.

"That boy," Granddaddy once announced to the family after watching me consume a Sunday dinner, "can eat more than any two buck niggers." His remark became something of a family joke, a constant reminder of my appetite and the esteem in which the family held the faceless black males who performed most of the hard labor in the community.

Granddaddy's behavior toward blacks puzzled me, for it contradicted the basic racial stereotypes and segregationist doctrines that I knew he held. It was his actions that confused me, for they often belied his sometimes heated racial rhetoric. Occasionally he would act in ways that actually defied the racial mores of the white community. This seeming inconsistency on racial matters fascinated me and increased my admiration of his uncompromising individualism.

From watching Granddaddy relate to Wade's blacks, I knew that he was genuinely fond of many of them. It was obvious that he enjoyed their company and respected them as persons. Just as clearly, many blacks, especially those of his generation, men and women who had known him for two decades or more, respected and admired him. Black farmers who were former neighbors, who had seen his child born and his home burned, came to Mr. Lonnie when times were hard to ask for credit or loans, even though they lived miles from the village and usually traded with closer merchants. They wanted, and expected, to see Granddaddy himself.

"Where your granddaddy, boy?" they would ask if I happened to be alone in the store. Or, "Where Mr. Lonnie?"—making it clear they had not come to talk with me.

"He's at lunch," or, "He's in town," I would explain.

"When he gone be back?" would come the inevitable response.

Informed of the time of his expected return, they would make a decision. "I'll wait right here for him," they would reply, or, "I'll come back tomorrow. You be sure and tell Mr. Lonnie I come, and that I'll be back tomorrow."

Often they came bearing gifts, something of their own, never anything store-bought: a bundle of turnips, a dozen eggs, a bushel of sweet potatoes. The really old friends would bring perhaps a jar of corn whiskey. Partially tokens of friendship, partially an offering to The Man, and perhaps partially a means of retaining some personal dignity and sense of worth while seeking favors, the offerings were always accepted. I never saw him dismiss an individual perfunctorily. He listened without interruption until their stories were told, and they seldom came away completely empty-handed.

On other occasions Granddaddy was less the patron holding court. He would often chat with older blacks, male and female, about good times past and hard times endured. In such conversations no favors were ever asked, and none were offered. He would converse for half an hour or more with people he had known for twenty or thirty years. I realized he enjoyed these people and felt some emotional attachment to them. Yet within minutes after the conversation, he might allow the failure of some hapless black to reduce his indebtedness to provoke a stream of profanity addressed to anyone who happened to be within earshot. Such contradictory behavior was not unusual, and certain extreme examples remain permanently etched into my racial consciousness, reminders of the complexity of segregation as it was practiced by those who, like Granddaddy, saw themselves as the guardians of at least certain members of the lesser race.

Viny Love presented a threat to no one. Perhaps the village's most paranoid racists—those few whites so insecure as to see all blacks as fools or knaves bent upon harming or deceiving whites at every opportunity—imagined that Viny could threaten their person or challenge their status. Most, however, accepted her for what she was, one of the earth's disinherited, a solitary figure engaged in a desperate struggle to support herself and her child, a woman who lived beyond the social structures and concern of even her own people. She was a shadowy figure, a strange, ugly woman, a black apparition who occasionally materialized to purchase groceries and household necessities, and then faded from sight and from the community's consciousness.

Viny made no effort to involve herself in the life of the community. She belonged to neither of Wade's two black churches and seldom attended religious services. If Jesus was her refuge, as he was for so many of Wade's women, black and white, she sought him in seclusion. She did not participate in black social activities. So far as I knew, she was never invited into any of the homes of the black families of the village and had no reason to attend events held at the black school. When in the village she kept to herself and was rarely seen speaking with anyone, black or white.

She lived about a mile from the village. Her house stood in a clearing surrounded by an imposing palisade formed by the straight trunks of longleaf pines. Dry, brown pine needles covered the sheet tin roof of the house and carpeted the otherwise barren earth of the yard. The house was constructed of unpainted heart pine weatherboarding, its tongue-and-groove planking disjointed with age. Rotting plank steps led to a bare front porch that ran across the front of the house and extended some eight or nine feet from the front door. Perched high above the ground on pillars of red brick, the building resembled some monstrous emaciated animal, its curtainless windows staring out vacantly at any who approached.

For as long as I could remember Viny had lived in this house with her only child, a boy about my age. I had never seen him, nor did I know anyone who had. He was the product of some past union about which I knew nothing. No one spoke of his father, not even in the ritual gossiping that occupied so much of the villagers' spare time. It was as if the boy had been spontaneously created, had materialized from nowhere, without the benefit of husband or lover. I had learned what little I knew about him from snatches of low-toned adult conversations that sometimes followed Viny's visits to the store. I knew that he had been damaged at birth, that he could neither walk nor talk, and that he never left the house. I knew that Viny kept him from the sight of others—not even my grandfather had seen him. I had heard black women muttering that the boy howled at night and speculating that an evil eye, some powerful curse, was responsible for his condition. I was never curious about him; he was a nonperson, without enough reality, enough presence, to arouse my curiosity.

While I, like the rest of Wade's residents, was but vaguely aware of the boy, he was the center of Viny Love's existence. Isolated from the community beyond the curious gaze of blacks and whites, she cared for the crippled child. She earned their living as a common field hand, laboring at tasks usually reserved for black men. In the spring she guided a plow through unbroken land with muscle-thickened arms. Even when she plowed, she was always dressed in a straight, knee-length skirt, her hair covered with either the upper portion of a worn stocking or a knotted bandanna. At the height of summer she worked in the tobacco fields with the men, stooping to break gold-green leaves from plant after plant. Only in the fall did she work with other women, dragging a large burlap bag slung from her shoulder between rows of mature cotton plants, picking the fiber from the bolls and stuffing the cotton into the bag until it was too heavy to be pulled. Then she had to empty the bag at the row's end and refill it in the same laborious manner.

Viny's occupation was not the one of her choice. Economic realities forced her into the fields, into tasks traditionally performed by men. Unlike many of Wade's domestic servants, Viny had no man to provide economic aid, no matter how little or how sporadic. Domestic labor paid less than the grueling tasks she performed, and so did the less strenuous agricultural jobs usually reserved for women. So Viny went into the fields. That action further separated her from the black community, and it also somehow desexed her.

It was hard for me to imagine that Viny had borne a child or to think of her as a mother. She certainly didn't look the part. I always thought of her in masculine terms, and so, I suspect, did the rest of the community. After years of strenuous field labor she looked masculine, despite her standard costume of skirt and sleeveless blouse. Her dark black skin, weathered by constant exposure to sun and wind, was stretched over heavily muscled limbs. I remember her forearms, with their well-defined muscles and the bulging blood vessels that ran just beneath the surface of the skin, the large, knotted calf muscles that lent her thin legs the appearance of brittle broomstaws that threatened to snap at each step. Her round face was expressionless, as if, convinced that emotions were useless in her struggle to survive, she had abandoned them years ago. To me it was an ugly face, without the slightest trace of feminine softness, its masculine appearance accentuated by a bulge of chewing tobacco in the cheek.

What I knew about Viny I had learned in the same way that I had learned about her son, from scattered bits of gossip, snatches of conversations between customers who remained at the store after Viny had come and gone. She visited the store infrequently, perhaps once a week during warm weather, less during the winter. When she came she said little except for the customary greeting, which she mumbled between lips stretched taut by the lump of tobacco in her cheek. With a single-minded purpose, in a flat, expressionless monotone, she ordered the items she had come to purchase. Her voice was steady and sure, indicating a quiet self-confidence. I knew that she was not among those blacks Granddaddy considered friends, that she had no personal connection to our family, no history of hard times shared, no record of domestic service in either McLaurin household. So far as I could determine, to Granddaddy she was just another of the community's black women, peculiar, withdrawn, viewed as an eccentric and therefore arousing some suspicion, but certainly no one to be concerned about, no one to demand special attention or to whom favors or even social recognition was owed.

I also knew that, without liking Viny, Granddaddy respected her. She had been a customer for years, buying groceries on credit and settling her debts in the summer and fall when agricultural jobs were plentiful. Because she was one of those blacks he judged worthy—those who had always paid their debts, never presented Wade's whites with problems, and posed no threat to the status quo—Granddaddy unhesitatingly honored her requests for extensions of credit or short advances of cash.

Probably because of her isolation, Viny, unlike many of Wade's black domestic laborers, had avoided the label of gossip, petty thief, or malingerer, all epithets whites frequently, and usually unjustly, pinned on their black employees. Such charges, of course, did not have to be factual. It was enough that they reflected the view that whites generally held of blacks. All blacks were assumed to be dishonest unless proven otherwise. Even years of faithful service could not completely dispel a white employer's belief that a servant would resort to theft. And whites defined as malingerers not those blacks who actually shunned work, but, rather, black employees who failed to work at the pace whites believed they should. That whites lacked experience at the tasks in question was somehow unrelated to their expectations. Viny, however, had proven herself. Despite her self-imposed isolation and the aura of mystery that isolation created around her, she was, by consensus, held to be "a good nigger," solid, dependable, and a good worker.

Viny came to Granddaddy that winter because she believed he appreciated, or at least respected, her years of labor and self-reliance, her efforts to obey the rules whites promulgated for black workers. She came hesitantly, as if unconvinced that her problems merited his attention, and only because circumstances left her no alternative. As soon as she entered the store I realized that this was not a usual visit. Her body had assumed the traditional posture of the supplicant; her eyes telegraphed the concerns that prompted her appearance. Although I knew she hadn't come to shop, I extended the expected greeting.

"Hello, Viny. What can I help you with today?"

She wasted no time with the usual southern pleasantries but instead got right to the point. "I wants to speak to Mr. Lonnie. Is he here?"

"He's outside. Wait a minute and I'll get him." I was accustomed to being ignored by older blacks, those who had adult business with Granddaddy, but there was a special sense of urgency in Viny's voice. I left through the back door to find Granddaddy stretched belly down across the front seat of his Chevrolet coupe, preoccupied with a malfunctioning heater.

"Granddaddy, Viny Love wants to see you."

"Well," he replied, not looking up from the heater, "what the hell does she want?"

"Didn't say. Just said she wants to talk with you."

"Son-of-a-bitch." He turned his torso and raised his head. "Tell her I'll be there in a minute."

I returned and did as I was instructed, and then took a seat behind the counter to wait for the next customer. None came. Viny waited patiently until Granddaddy came in.

"Hello, Viny. How're you doing?"

"Not so good, Mr. Lonnie, not too good at all."

"The boy said you want to talk with me, so what can I do for you? Got no problems, I hope."

"Yes, sir, Mr. Lonnie, I shore do. It's my boy worries me most. You know work's hard to come by this time of the year, Mr. Lonnie, and I just can't get enough to buy what he needs. I applied for the welfare 'bout two months ago. Didn't have no other choice, Mr. Lonnie, and that's the truth. They said they'd send along somebody, but nobody's come yet. I don't know what to do. Can you ask 'em to come out here? God knows I don't mean to trouble you none, but you knows I need the help, otherwise I wouldn't ask. Can you ask 'em, Mr. Lonnie?"

"It won't be any trouble, Viny, be glad to do what I can. I'll call Wilson at the welfare office today. But you'll need some things now, I suspect. Just tell the boy what you want. Don't worry about the money right now, you just pay me when you can."

"Yes, sir, Mr. Lonnie. I shore do thank you. I shore do."

Granddaddy acknowledged her thanks without words, briefly nodding his head in her direction, then returned to his work on the car's heater. I abandoned my perch to fill Viny's order of canned goods and staples. Within minutes she left the store, a bag of groceries cradled in each arm.

That night Viny's plight was incorporated into the general conversation of Granddaddy's friends, a mixed crew of farmers, tradesmen, and a few clerical workers and civil service employees who held jobs at Fayetteville and Fort Bragg. Granddaddy brought up the subject, condemning the bureaucratic inefficiency of the welfare department.

"Viny Love was in here today," he announced to the group at large. Viny needed no introduction to his audience. They all knew her and the difficulties she faced. "Seems she's applied for welfare but can't get a case worker out to see if she qualifies. That's typical. Them that deserves help can't get it."

"Well, if any nigger qualifies, she does," volunteered Henry Eason. "That's a hard-working nigger woman, sure enough." Henry spoke from experience. Viny had cultivated his cornfields and harvested his cotton and tobacco for years. "I ain't never heard nobody say Viny wouldn't work. Damn shame she ain't being helped, what with half the sorry niggers in Wade on some kind of welfare."

"That's the god's truth." Vernon Moore, a heavyset middle-aged man whose bearlike body seemed appropriate for a diesel mechanic, picked up the theme. "You take that Evans woman. I hear she draws a check for herself and her three little niggers. Her ole man don't hit a lick of work. Claims he's a brickmason but he lays damn few bricks."

"George Evans's a no-account son-of-a-bitch," Granddaddy agreed. "The bastard's been owing me money for over three years. Most of the time he's too goddamned drunk to lay bricks. Son-of-a-bitch lives off of Dorthea's welfare. Claims they're separated and he don't live with her. And poor Viny Love, she's out there busting her ass, and when she can't get work the goddamned welfare people won't even talk to her. It just ain't right."

"Lonnie, you know damn well you can't expect the welfare people to be fair." Henry Eason seemed surprised that Granddaddy could have entertained the thought. "Ain't any of that bunch works none too hard either. Probably be another week before they send somebody."

"Well," Granddaddy continued, claiming the last word on the subject. "I called James Wilson today. He said he'd try to get out here within a couple of days. We'll see."

James Wilson was one of those people I saw at the store about once every four months or so but didn't really know. He was the caseworker the welfare department assigned to interview prospective clients in our area of the county. Since Granddaddy knew most of the region's blacks, Wilson usually stopped at the store seeking directions to the homes of black welfare applicants and to ask routine questions about their general reputation, income, and property holdings. He was the quintessential bureaucrat, and I despised him. He was a little sharp-faced man, his balding head surrounded by a fringe of closely cropped graying hair, his paunch and spreading backsides betraying the sedentary nature of his occupation. He always seemed ill at ease, moving about jerkily as if the starched high-collar shirts he wore made him uncomfortable.

Several days after Granddaddy's call, Wilson stopped at the store. I was alone, reading to kill time, and resented having to abandon my book for someone I so disliked. Wilson ordered a Coke, popped his index finger in the bottle top a couple of times, then began with the business at hand.

"You know a woman named Viny Love?"

"Yes, sir."

"Known her long?"

"Yes, sir. Ever since I can remember."

Wilson would drink a swallow of Coke between questions, popping his finger in the bottle top after each gulp. "She married?"

"No, sir, not as I know of."

"Live with anybody?"

"No, sir, least I never heard she did."

He paused a moment, as if satisfied with my responses to his questions about Viny's morality, then moved to the next topic of his inquiry.

"You know her boy?"

"No, sir. I know she's got one, but I've never seen him."

"You know who's the boy's father?"

"No, sir."

Wilson finished his Coke, sat the bottle on the counter and looked out the window as if contemplating my answers. Throughout the interview he had projected an air of indifference, as if my responses were of no consequence, all the while fiddling with the Coke bottle and gazing at the rows of shelved merchandise, never facing me. "Well," he said, continuing to look through the window at nothing in particular, "I guess I had better go see this Viny Love." Wilson turned from the window, looked down at his feet, then up at me. "Where does she live, boy?"

"See that road between the store and the school? Go down it, about a mile 'til the road runs out. Viny's house is at the end of the road, back up in some pines."

Wilson nodded, then smiled for the first time, satisfied that he could find the place. "Where's your granddaddy? I thought he'd be here this afternoon."

"I don't know. He comes and goes pretty much as he pleases when I'm here."

"Well, you tell him I came about Viny Love. Be sure and do that, you hear me, boy?"

"Yes, sir, I'll be sure to tell him." I started to add that Grand-daddy would probably return within an hour or so, but Wilson had stepped through the door and was headed for his automobile.

That evening I told Granddaddy about Wilson's visit and the questions he had asked. Granddaddy seemed unconcerned about Wilson's appearance, which he probably expected. He grunted to acknowledge my information and made no comment, failed even to ask the nature of Wilson's inquiries. For weeks after that brief non-exchange neither Granddaddy nor anyone else mentioned Viny Love, nor did I see her at the store. Granddaddy had performed what he considered to be his duty; he had honored Viny's request. His telephone call had informed the authorities of Viny's predicament. As a man accustomed to having his word accepted without question, he expected the welfare department to act on the information he had provided. As a southern white who believed in "looking out" for blacks judged deserving, he assumed that Viny would receive aid, and receive it quickly. To Granddaddy, who acted from a code of personal obligation, any other response to what he considered an obvious case of need was unthinkable.

That the welfare department shared neither Granddaddy's code of personal obligation nor his sense of immediacy became evident with Viny's second appeal for help. He was seated next to the heater in his favorite chair, an overstuffed armchair covered with yellow-green plastic, when Viny entered the store.

"Cold out today, ain't it, Viny," he greeted her, expecting Viny to respond to his greeting, then inform him of a successful interview with Wilson.

"Yes, sir, it sure is that," Viny responded, then hesitated.

"Wilson come out to see you, did he?"

Again, Viny made no effort to continue.

Granddaddy nodded, reassured by what he assumed to be Viny's positive reply. Things were on schedule, rewards were forthcoming to the good and faithful. "Got your check, have you?" he asked.

Viny lowered her head as she answered, as if ashamed to disappoint him. "No, sir, I ain't, Mr. Lonnie. That's what I've come to talk with you about. That Mr. Wilson, he come to the house all right, asked a heap of questions. I showed him the boy, then he left. He said I'd hear something soon, but I ain't heard nothing yet, Mr. Lonnie. Now I hardly got nothing to feed the boy, and no money. Mr. Lonnie, ain't there something you can do?"

Viny's sad, desperate outburst took Granddaddy by surprise; he had expected Viny to report that she had received a check, or at least that aid had been promised and would soon arrive. His expectations shattered, he was furious. He felt Viny had been unjustly treated by an incompetent bureaucrat, and he felt personally betrayed. His recommendations had been ignored. The welfare department had failed to aid someone he had designated as deserving, a failure he certainly interpreted as a direct affront to his integrity. Such a challenge to his personal honor was intolerable. I could see his facial muscles tighten, his eyebrows move downward to meet the bridge of his nose, his face flush ever so slightly—all signs that Granddaddy was about to take action.

"Your boy home?" he asked Viny, his voice hard, flat, filled with a controlled fury I had learned to recognize by a slightly higher pitch.

"Why, yes, sir, he to the house," Viny replied, surprised at the question.

"Boy," Granddaddy called to me across the store, completely ignoring Viny, "go see if Theo's home. If he's there, bring him here. Tell him I want him right now. Not tomorrow, right now, goddammit, you hear."

"Yes, sir." I heard. I knew Granddaddy was enraged, that he intended to retaliate against Wilson. I had no idea of his plans, and caution overwhelmed my curiosity. This was not the time to question him about his intentions. Instead I left the store, crossed the highway and ran down the dirt path that led to Theo's house, which was visible from the storefront windows.

Theo lived there with his mother, Marietta Davis. His father had died years ago and Theo, now in his late twenties, supported himself and his mother by working at the sawmill and tending the few acres of land behind their home, which he planted each year in vegetables and corn. He was a huge, awkward black man, an awe-inspiring figure on a basketball court, where, the store excepted, I saw Theo most. His presence on a team meant an automatic victory. At six feet eight, perhaps more, and easily weighing 240 pounds, Theo controlled without challenge both offensive and defensive backboards. The kids, black and white, viewed him as a local Wilt Chamberlain. The white kids especially seldom thought of him as anything other than a basketball player. He had the personality of a koala bear. Black kids loved him, whites respected him. He was one of the few blacks I had never heard anyone speak ill of.

I approached Marietta's house, hoping that Theo would be home, because I knew Granddaddy would be enraged if I came back without him. I walked up the walkway of pine straw that led to the porch and knocked on the front door, keeping a wary eye on two large mixed-breed dogs that crawled from beneath the house to bark at the intruder. It was only half past three, but by some stroke of luck Theo was home. He came to the door and quieted the dogs.

"Theo," I gasped breathlessly, not waiting for his recognition or welcome, "Granddaddy wants you to come to the store. He said he wants you right now."

"Something the matter? What does Mr. Lonnie want?"

"I don't know—it's got something to do with Viny Love. All I know is he wants you there now."

Theo ducked back into the house for a moment and emerged struggling to get into an old blue suede jacket. We hurried back to the store, Theo all the while plying me with questions for which I had no answers. Granddaddy met us with his Chevrolet just as we crossed the highway. He had seen us coming and had closed the store. Inside the car I could see Viny seated in the back. Granddaddy stopped the car, leaned across the seat and opened the door. "You two get in," he ordered. Without a word Theo climbed into the back seat with Viny, tucking his long legs, while I got in front with Granddaddy. By then I knew we were going to Viny Love's, but I wasn't sure why.

Granddaddy volunteered no answers for questions I knew better than to ask. He said nothing until we reached Viny's house, not a word to Theo about his intentions, nothing to Viny about his plans. Of course, he might have talked with Viny while I had gone to get Theo, but if Viny knew anything, she also remained silent.

When we reached Viny's house Granddaddy parked at the front steps, opened his door, slid from behind the steering wheel and began issuing what he would have termed requests, but I interpreted as orders. "Viny, you take Theo into the house and get your boy. Theo, you go in with Viny and bring the boy out here. Then put him in the back seat." Viny and Theo did as they were told without question or hesitation, though their faces registered momentary surprise. Within minutes Viny emerged from the house followed by Theo, who cradled the boy in his arms.

For an instant after catching sight of the boy Granddaddy's face revealed the shock we both felt. His light skin should have come as no surprise, for light-skinned blacks were no rarity in Wade, yet neither of us had considered the possibility that his father might have been white. Viny, we assumed, was too hard, too masculine, too ugly, too *negro* to have attracted a white man. Nor were we prepared for the severity of the boy's handicaps. He was the first victim of severe cerebral palsy I had ever seen, and I thought him barely human. His legs dangled helplessly over Theo's left arm, like those of some life-sized rag doll, bouncing loosely against Theo's left thigh with each step he took. His head rolled back to rest on Theo's right shoulder, his twisted arms were held tightly against his chest, hands limply folded just under the chin, as if held in an agonizing prayer. His frail body, which appeared weightless in Theo's huge arms, was stuffed into a plaid wool shirt and a frayed pair of jeans. Despite the near freezing weather, he wore no jacket. His eyes reflected the fear he felt, helpless in the arms of a stranger, removed from the security of his world, gawked at by whites he had never seen. A forlorn, desperate cry gurgled up from his throat, causing Viny to move toward him.

Viny's movement distracted our attention from the boy, who for a moment had held us transfixed, stunned somehow by the reality that was at the heart of Viny's daily existence. His composure regained, Granddaddy reasserted his control of the situation. "Viny, get in the back seat." He spoke in a less demanding tone but still managed to convey the impression that he expected no arguments. Viny hesitated briefly and then left Theo and the boy and moved over to Granddaddy who held the front seat forward and helped her climb into the car. "Now, Theo, put the boy in the back with Viny." Theo leaned down into the automobile and gently deposited the boy next to his mother. "Now you two sit up front with me," Granddaddy said, motioning for us to walk around to the right side of the car. I slipped into the automobile first, and Theo followed, closing the door as Granddaddy turned the ignition switch.

Although it felt like hours, the drive to Fayetteville took no more than thirty minutes. Each house, each familiar curve along the way crawled by and, once passed, seemed like weights attached to the vehicle, exerting a pull that delayed our progress. We crept down the road in silence. I was sandwiched between Granddaddy, whom I tried not to touch for fear I would interfere with his driving, and Theo's enormous legs, which filled half the seat. Wedged between them, I could not turn around to observe Viny and the boy, and would have been reluctant to do so in any case. Granddaddy and Theo looked straight down the road, their heads motionless, as if looking to either the left or right would somehow divert us from our destination. From the back seat came the boy's incomprehensible cries, followed by Viny's softspoken assurance, those shushes and hummings used by mothers everywhere to calm frightened children, the universal sounds of love and protection. It all seemed so unreal—me sitting between my grandfather and a giant basketball player while a weather-hardened, muscled female field hand in the backseat stroked, petted, and crooned lullabyes to a terrified crippled child, all of us in a 1953 Chevrolet headed for the Cumberland County Department of Welfare.

At exactly 4:30, Granddaddy pulled into a reserved parking place directly in front of the office of the welfare department. "Theo," he said, opening his door, "you come around here." "Boy, he continued, addressing me, "you get out of the car. Viny, I want you out, too."

Theo eased himself out of the car and walked around to Granddaddy's door. I followed him. Granddaddy stood holding the back of his seat forward so Viny could get out of the coupe.

"Theo, get the boy." Granddaddy pressed the back of his seat forward even more, giving Theo room to maneuver. Theo bent forward from the waist, reached into the back seat and picked up the child, who again began to utter his frightened noises. As Theo straightened up, the boy in his arms, Viny stepped up to take hold of the child's hand and comfort him.

Granddaddy shut the car door. "Theo, you and Viny follow me. Boy," he continued, addressing me, "you stay here with the car."

I watched the four of them, Granddaddy in the lead, march up the white concrete sidewalk and enter the two-story red brick structure that housed the offices of the welfare department. I felt betrayed because, having come this far, I was forbidden to go further. I was humiliated because I had been ordered to watch the car, clearly an insignificant task, and furious because I was going to miss what promised to be a rousing confrontation inside. I knew, however, that this was neither the time nor the place to question Granddaddy's instructions, and that I would have to be content with hearing the events of the next few minutes related to me later.

I had to wait until the next day to learn what had happened, for the long drive home—Viny in the back seat singing to her son and Granddaddy, Theo, and I squeezed into the front—proved as silent as the trip up.

Theo knew, of course, that I would be dying to hear a blow-by-blow account of Granddaddy's confrontation with the welfare bureaucracy and came to the store to deliver it.

"Yes, sir, boy, you missed it," Theo began his tale by reminding me of my juvenile status. "You shore enough missed it. Let me have a pack of Camels."

Obviously Theo intended to amuse himself at the expense of my curiosity, and obviously I could do little to prevent him. So I handed him the cigarettes, took the quarter he offered in payment, and waited. He toyed with my anxiety, carefully and slowly removing the cellophane from the top of the pack, extracting a cigarette, and then lighting it. He exhaled the smoke of his first puff.

"Your Granddaddy, boy, he's something. Yes, sir, that man's something else." Theo shook his head, as if Granddaddy's actions were beyond belief, but said nothing else.

"Well," I said, no longer able to control my impatience, "what the hell happened?"

Satisfied that he had sufficiently whetted my curiosity, Theo began to recite his version of events of the day before.

"Mr. Lonnie, he told us to stay right with him, no matter what, an' we did. He goes right through the door an' up to this white lady at a desk an' asks where Mr. McPherson's office is. McPherson, he be the big man at the welfare. That lady say Mr. McPherson's office is just down the hall, but that it was too late, and besides Mr. Lonnie would need an appointment. All the time they be talking, I'm standing holding the boy, Viny right beside me. Well, then, Mr. Lonnie, he just ignored that woman, turn around to me an' say to follow him, an' we do. That lady, she jumps up an' says we can't go in there, but Mr. Lonnie don't pay her no mind."

Theo interrupted his narrative to puff on his cigarette, slowly exhaling an elongated blue cloud of smoke which disintegrated as it floated lazily across the room, then continued.

"Mr. Lonnie, he walk straight to McPherson's office, me following with the boy and Viny, her holding on to his arm. Mr. Lonnie open the door an' we walk right in. McPherson, he be sittin' in a big chair behind his desk, an' he looks up at us like he don't know what in the world's happening. Mr. Lonnie don't say nothing to McPherson, not one word, he just turns to me an' say, 'Theo, put that boy down on the desk' an' I did, I set him down right in front of McPherson, on top of papers an' everything. By this time, McPherson he starts to say something but Mr. Lonnie cuts him right off. I mean he blessed the man out. He says Viny's a hard-working, honest woman, but she needs some help. Says Wilson seen the boy weeks ago, still they ain't heard nothing from the welfare. He tell McPherson to look at that boy an' say he don't need help, asks how can the welfare refuse to help somebody who needs it so bad. Then he say if something's not done, damned if he don't take the boy to the county commissioners an' see what they can do."

"My God!" I interrupted Theo, unable to refrain from expressing my excitement and more disappointed than ever that I had missed the main event. "What did McPherson say then?"

Theo paused at my question to take another drag off his cigarette and then continued, caught up in his own narrative and no longer bothering to keep up the suspense.

"He say to Mr. Lonnie that if he would get the boy out of his office, maybe they could work something out. So Mr. Lonnie told us to go wait in the lobby, but not to go outside unless he said so. So I took the boy out there an' set him in a chair. Viny, she set down next to him. All them office workers, they stared at the boy something awful, but we just waited. Mr. Lonnie, he stay in with McPherson about ten or fifteen minutes. Then he come out, told me to bring the boy back to the car. Didn't say nothing else. I shore would like to have heard what them two said."

"Yeah, me too." Theo ended his tale with exactly my thoughts. "Not likely Granddaddy's going to tell us, though. Guess we'll just have to wait and see what happens."

"You're right about that," Theo agreed. "Well, guess I'll go. Your Granddaddy's a good man, boy. You know, I don't believe he's afraid of nobody. That man's something else."

Theo left me to think of Granddaddy and Viny Love and the boy. I knew that few other whites, perhaps none, would have done what Granddaddy did for Viny Love. Some might have spoken with McPherson about her, if asked to do so, but none would have taken such drastic action. My grandfather was, as Theo had said, something else, an original, and I knew it. I was tremendously proud of his actions, yet puzzled by them. I didn't understand how he could so outrageously flout accepted standards of behavior on behalf of a black, even a good black, while simultaneously subscribing to segregationist doctrines and racist beliefs. His efforts on Viny's behalf helped instill in me the concept that on occasion one was expected to risk social censure on behalf of blacks, that they, too, were human, with rights and feelings we were bound to respect. Yet, on the other hand, I realized that Granddaddy saw blacks as somehow incapable of fending for themselves. Granddaddy perceived blacks as humans who were irrevocably flawed.

At the time I was too in awe of Granddaddy to understand that he had not acted solely because of his desire to help Viny, that, to some degree, he had acted because his word had been challenged. He had told Wilson that Viny needed aid, he had asked Wilson to consider her case, and he had told Viny that he had talked to Wilson. Not only had his word been questioned but, as he saw it, when no aid was forthcoming, his position of authority as a link between dependent blacks and the county bureaucracy was challenged. At sixteen, I lacked the experience to understand such complex motives and assumed Granddaddy had taken such drastic action to right what he perceived as an injustice, that he had acted out of concern for Viny and her boy and for no other reason.

After more than twenty-five years of reflecting upon that episode, I have a better understanding of the complexity of his motives, but am still uncertain as to the significance, the weight that he assigned to each of them. Given the rules and regulations of segregation and the realities of life under the system, I doubt that even Granddaddy knew.

Jerry and Miss Carrie

As proponents of an ideology of hatred and fear, Wade's white segregationists relied heavily on stereotypes to support their claim that blacks were inferior. They also exercised their power within the society to see that the image of blacks that they created became a reality. Blacks, they maintained, were incapable of economic progress without white sponsors, unable to administer organizations or institutions successfully without white help, and generally unfit to hold positions of authority. In the South's economy, they noted, blacks were domestics, tenants, day laborers, hewers of wood and drawers of water. To ensure that this situation would remain unchanged, they denied blacks entry into the professions, the business world, and managerial positions. Whites bemoaned the lack of effective black leaders, but at the same time, in order to make sure that there were none, they barred blacks not just from positions of leadership, but from participation in the community's political and social institutions.

Because whites met few blacks whose social or economic status challenged segregationist dogma, the racial stereotypes employed in this circular rationale were devastatingly effective. Most rural and small-town whites, who, like residents of Wade, were segregation's most ardent defenders, rarely encountered black professionals, businessmen, or other members of the black middle class that had sprung up in larger southern cities despite the restrictions of segregation. Before entering college I had never known a black doctor, lawyer, academician, or businessman. Except for a few black teachers and the principal of the local black elementary school, a light-skinned man in his fifties who lived in Fayetteville and was addressed by the members of Wade's black community as "Professor," all the blacks I knew personally were, in economic terms, decidedly lower class.

Yet the practical considerations of daily life in Wade, as elsewhere in the South, demanded close contact between blacks and whites. Partly because of these personal contacts, whites insisted they they held no animosity toward blacks. Instead, they professed to like blacks and boasted of having always "gotten along" well with them. They supported segregation, they explained, because it was in the best interests of and preferred by members of both races. Like Orville Faubus and George Wallace, the white people of Wade never claimed that their best friends were Negroes, only that they were the Negroes' best friend.

Northern critics greeted such assertions with laughter or disbelief, sometimes both, and dismissed them as self-serving rhetoric. Unfortunately, this only convinced Wade's whites of northern hypocrisy because they knew of conditions in northern urban ghettoes, and because their segregationist beliefs were not merely self-serving. The tenacity with which Wade's residents and other southerners defended segregation while insisting with equal fervor that they enjoyed warm personal relationships with individual blacks cannot be easily dismissed. Perhaps whites consciously lied about their attitude toward blacks, both as a group and as individuals. Perhaps, as some have suggested, blacks presented a pleasant face to whites as a coping mechanism, when in actuality they held whites in contempt. My experiences as a youth, however, indicate that whites believed blacks inferior but at the same time responded to them as individuals on an emotional level that contradicted, at least temporarily, their racist assumptions.

Everyday life in the South argued persuasively for this last possibility. While whites rarely encountered "successful" blacks, personal relations with black individuals constantly produced situations and experiences that undermined the segregationist's stereotypical view of blacks. The white residents of Wade occasionally encountered blacks who, despite their subordinate economic and social status, did not fit the segregationist mold. They also realized that even a moderately successful, independent black created doubts about segregation. So they increased their efforts to see that blacks remained in subservient positions, just as the proslavery theorists of the Old South had attempted to eliminate free Negroes because their very existence threatened the ideological framework on which slavery rested.

Many of the blacks I knew defied in some way the racial stereotypes of the segregationists. Street presented the greatest challenge to my traditionally racist beliefs, but Street was unique, a free spirit who operated beyond the bounds of the society in practically every area of life. It was not Street alone, however, who threatened the society's racial stereotypes. Other blacks I knew, more typical blacks, contributed to my growing doubts about segregation and to the emotional turmoil those doubts created. Observing them, I began to comprehend that blacks viewed whites quite differently than we viewed ourselves. Such knowledge they revealed inadvertently, in bits and pieces over a period of years. To a white southern youth in the mid-1950s who had been indoctrinated with the myth that "better whites" were the blacks' best friends, each such revelation came as a shock.

It was possible for whites, if they cared to do so, to learn how blacks perceived them. Blacks revealed their feelings in private moments, through unguarded remarks, and through impetuous acts. Often, however, such words or deeds were prompted by anger or frustration and were quickly disavowed. For a black in Wade to have challenged openly and directly the segregationist regime would have been unthinkable, at least before the end of the decade. To express resentment openly, even in jest, could have proved fatal. My initial comprehension of that basic reality came one day while listening to Daddy relate what he considered a humorous story to friends at the store.

His tale involved an encounter between Elliot Ray and Bill

Williams. Elliot was well known in Wade. I had often heard him called "the ugliest nigger" in town. My mother, despite the fact that she liked Elliot, often said that upon seeing him fright was her first reaction. He was jet black, a large man of average height, with a head and face disproportionately large for his body. His snaggled, gold-capped teeth did nothing to soften his facial features. Large, bulging eyes enhanced an already grotesque appearance. By any standards, Elliot qualified as ugly. He was, however, a marvelous person, kind, outgoing, and pleasant.

Bill Williams, who owned a farm outside Wade, was, if anything, uglier than Elliot. He always seemed in need of a shave and dressed in scruffy, oversized coveralls. A small, stooped man, his pinched, narrow face gave him a mean look accentuated by the fixed squint of a glass left eye. Bill never attained Elliot's reputation as a fine fellow, and for good reason.

One fall Saturday Elliot spied Bill in the sawmill commissary, where many mill hands purchased groceries. Both men already had begun their ritual of weekend drinking. Elliot, who had known Bill his entire life, for some inexplicable reason on this occasion burst into laughter upon catching sight of him across the room.

"I declare, Mr. Bill," Elliot boomed out over the crowd, "people say I be the ugliest nigger in Wade. Well, if that's so, you shore God the ugliest white man."

Elliot's good-humored but ill-advised observation enraged Bill. "I'll kill you, you black son-of-a-bitch. Ain't no goddamned nigger gonna call me ugly." Bill lunged through the crowd, determined to drive home and fetch his gun. "If you're here when I get back, you're one dead nigger."

The room divided into two groups, blacks and whites, as cooler heads in both camps tried to defuse the situation. Blacks whisked Elliot from the commissary and into someone's home, hoping that Bill would recover from his embarrassment and that his anger would subside. Whites kept Bill from his car, assuring him that Elliot had meant no harm, that it was just the liquor talking. They prevailed, and Bill went home, his anger reduced to a nonlethal level, and the incident was over.

Daddy's friends thought the incident hilarious and almost fell over themselves laughing. Elliot was right, they joked, even if he was a fool to say so. The potential for violence past, the entire episode could be treated as a lark. Yet I knew, as did the men who laughed so hard, that it had been no lark. I knew that had Bill Williams carried a gun in his car, as many of Wade's citizens did, Elliot probably would have been killed. As I realized, an effort to deny that reality had provoked the laughter. And their laughter, such a natural and wholesome extension of the daily ritual of conversation among friends, helped me see that denial of ultimate realities was essential to a segregated society, so long as the denial was plausible or, as in this case, pleasurable.

In the episode Daddy related, Bill Williams had learned in public how a single black perceived him, and that lesson had almost cost Elliot his life. Such public exchanges, had they occurred often, would have destroyed segregation. For that reason they were not tolerated when they did occur. Private revelations, however, were inevitable and more frequent. Yet because whites only perceived individually how they were viewed by individual blacks, the public image of race relations, the collective image of segregation, remained unchallenged. Each white southerner dealt with his newly acquired knowledge alone, as best he could. For me the recognition that blacks held less than complimentary views of whites, and of my family, resulted from a chance encounter with Dora Lou Smith.

Dora Lou was an unlikely source of revelation. Dora Lou and her family were among Wade's poorest blacks; they would hardly have qualified for inclusion at the bottom of most social and economic indices. Dora Lou lived a wretched life. Lloyd, her husband of some thirty years, was a broken logger, his body worn out by bouts with tuberculosis and the cumulative effects of accidents on the job. His was the fate of many of Wade's older black males. Used up, their productivity as laborers spent, they were cast aside, without pensions or support, deprived of elemental human dignity, a burden to their families. A beaten man, Lloyd had long ago relinquished direction of the family affairs to his more vigorous wife.

The Smiths had two children. The oldest, named for his father but called Jimbo by the community, was barely literate: he had attended school sporadically and had quit at the earliest opportunity. (In the segregated South school officials rarely worried about truant blacks.) Jimbo, who was in his early twenties, contributed little to the family's finances. If he could find work, he toiled as a day laborer on surrounding farms. When the demand for farm laborers fell in the winter, Jimbo spent most of his time at home.

Jimbo's sister, Jenny, added to Dora Lou's already considerable burdens. A year or so younger than Jimbo, she had contracted polio as a child. The illness had paralyzed her left side, withering her limbs and contorting her facial features. She walked with a pronounced limp, dragging her small, misshapen left leg. Her left arm, crooked at the elbow, the hand pointing upward, she carried clutched against her side. The fingers of the hand were rigid, yet she managed to hold larger objects between arm and body, balancing them on her hip. Jenny ignored her physical limitations. She was a common sight in the village, shuffling along its streets intent upon reaching some private destination.

Whatever the cause—her childhood bout with polio, a birth defect, or a random genetic malfunction—Jenny had the mental ability of a young school child. The paralysis had affected her speech, making her seem yet more retarded. Still, most of the time she functioned well enough to care for herself. Her mental abilities, whatever their extent, went undeveloped. Jenny had never attended school or received special training. Even if physical therapy or remedial education had been available to her, her parents could not have paid the price. So Jenny remained essentially illiterate, ignorant of her own possibilities, a crippled child-woman.

Her withered limbs, contorted face, and slurred speech marked her as an outcast. Yet she was normal enough to arouse neither pity nor concern among the village residents. Most ignored Jenny; she was but another part of the village landscape. As a retarded cripple, however, she was at the mercy of the most vicious and exploitative members of a mean and impoverished world. At sixteen she delivered a child, which no father acknowledged. Herself a child, Jenny presented her mother with the responsibility for yet another family member, a child whom fate would drag through life.

Dora Lou, in spite of the family's circumstances, was a marvel. A great yellow woman, a robust earth mother whose short, rotund body seemed to roll along unsupported by legs, she exuded strength and energy. Her strength carried the family, fused them into a single unit, and enabled them to survive. Hers was of necessity a physical strength, derived from dragging cotton-filled sacks between rows of white-bolled plants, from hoeing crops under a summer sun, from cleaning other people's houses and washing other people's clothes, from lifting babies and butchering hogs, from persevering.

Though beset by adversity, Dora Lou radiated an aura of impish serenity. She projected an indomitable will to survive and to do so with dignity. She engaged life with an unflappable sense of humor, as if instinctively aware that a serious outlook could be fatal. Dora Lou used laughter as a weapon, holding reality at bay by treating life as a pleasant joke, or at worst as a benign prank. Her cheerful façade disarmed whites, gained her room to maneuver. She understood that Wade's whites appreciated a "happy nigger" and believed that "their niggers" should be happy, and she used that knowledge to her advantage. Dora Lou never begged or pleaded; she clowned—always, I would learn, with a purpose. She was the classic fool.

For years I believed the character she played to be the real Dora Lou. But one day a conversation I overheard between her and Cooter, Jenny's boy, shattered my naive view of race relations, as well as my view of Dora Lou's character. I was about fourteen then, Cooter was preschool age, and God only knew how old Dora Lou was. She seemed unaffected by the passage of time, immune to the aging process. I had always known her, and while others had changed, acquired wrinkles or developed a bit of a stoop, Dora Lou had remained the same.

Like many of Wade's black women, Dora Lou occasionally worked as a domestic for my family. She sometimes cleaned and washed for both Mother and Ma Ma. Granddaddy employed her to give the store's restrooms a daily cleaning. It was not unusual for Dora Lou to bring Cooter with her to either home or store and to watch him while she worked.

The store's restrooms were not in the store, but in a separate building behind it. This wooden structure housed a pump room, with a large electric pump that also supplied water to the store. At the other end of the structure were the restrooms, each designated for the appropriate sex.

One day as I was about to leave the men's room, the clanging of buckets and harsh commands to a child who, despite his age, was expected to help with the cleaning, announced the entry of Dora Lou and Cooter into the adjacent women's room. What caught my attention, however, was not merely their presence, but Cooter's excited cry.

"Look, Mama. Look what I've found. I've found some money, Mama." Cooter always addressed Dora Lou as Mama and Jenny as Jenny.

"Come here, boy," I heard Dora Lou respond. "Just where do you think you're going?"

"I'm going to tell Mr. Lonnie, Mama."

"You bring that money to me right now." Dora Lou's voice, filled with anger, lashed out at the child.

For a moment the room next door fell silent and I assumed that Cooter did as he had been ordered. When Dora Lou spoke again the anger had disappeared from her voice, replaced by the knowing tone of a parent instructing a child about life's unfortunate realities.

"You find any money, boy, don't you say nothin' to nobody. You understand me? You put it in your pocket and bring it to me, and you keep your mouth shut. You hear me, boy?"

"Yes, ma'am," Cooter replied a bit hesitantly. "But what about Mr. Lonnie? Ain't I supposed to tell Mr. Lonnie about the money?"

"Don't you tell Mr. Lonnie nothin'. Don't you never say nothin' to him about that money." The anger again cracked through Dora Lou's voice. "That white man's got plenty of money, boy. More money than he know what to do with. We ain't got nothin'. What you finds, you keep. You best remember that."

Sounds of splashing water and brush bristles scouring tile walls signaled the end of Dora Lou's lecture. She had resumed her cleaning. Seizing this opportunity to escape without her spotting me and realizing that I had overheard her advice to Cooter, I left the men's room and quickly returned to the store.

The brief pang of guilt I felt about eavesdropping was suddenly replaced by outrage. How *dare* Dora Lou tell Cooter not to inform my grandfather of money lost on his property? Granddaddy was no thief; he was an honorable man, and everyone knew it. He would do the right thing, see that the money was returned to anyone reporting its loss or, in the absence of such a claim, return it to Dora Lou. Her advice contradicted the ethics I had been taught by my family, the Presbyterian Sunday school, my teachers, and the village elders, and was an affront to my sense of honor and honesty. What disturbed me most, however, was the anger in her voice as she spoke of Granddaddy. The very idea that she did not trust him, would withhold information from him, infuriated me. Suddenly I not only realized that blacks saw Granddaddy much differently than I did, but I also began to grasp the significance of that difference in perspective. Granddaddy was not universally admired; by some he was viewed not just with occasional anger but with permanent mistrust and envy, perhaps even hatred. My initial response to that insight was to condemn blacks as ingrates, unworthy of Granddaddy's attention. Time and experience would change that original verdict.

While I grew toward a future that was unattainable, even unimaginable for them, the Smith family remained unchanged. Gradually I came to understand that they were lost—judged failures and written off by the society of which I was a part. I realized that perhaps the most significant difference between the Smiths and my family was that I had a future, a future with all the options and rewards that the word connotes. While I remained in Wade, Dora Lou was a constant reminder of the conversation I had overheard, of the fact that some blacks perceived Granddaddy, perhaps my entire family, as the Enemy. By the time I left home I understood that Dora Lou's view of us was, given her perspective, as close to the truth as the concept we held of ourselves.

Dora Lou's revelation further shattered my traditional paternalistic image of race relations. Associations with other blacks would scatter the bits and pieces of that fragmented mosaic. These pleasant associations at first appeared to preserve the old pattern. For the most part they involved blacks who posed no threat to the status quo or who, unlike Street, said little to challenge my intellectual curiosity. They were with people I enjoyed talking to, with whom I held the simple, seemingly meaningless conversations that were nevertheless powerful agents binding the community into a single social unit. Except for Street, there was no one I enjoyed talking with more than Jerome Walters.

Jerome, who was Granddaddy's age, was a retired mill hand who had scraped together the funds to purchase the small frame house in which he lived. His wife had died years before I met him, and he never remarried. He was a wiry little man, stooped by years, yet his lively eyes reflected his continued enjoyment of life. Jerome lived with Martha, a daughter who was in her mid-thirties. Martha was lighter than Jerome, an earthy, radiantly sensuous woman of commanding presence. She worked at Fort Bragg and added a measure of financial independence to her father's retirement. Later she would marry a staff sergeant; after her marriage Jerome's house remained the home of the enlarged family.

Jerome usually came to the store once or twice during the week and every Saturday. He often stayed for as much as an hour, greeting other blacks, talking with Daddy or Granddaddy and, if I wasn't too busy, with me. We always talked sports, especially baseball. A rabid Yankee fan, Jerome was a rarity among Wade's black sports buffs, since the Yankees then had no black players. Other black baseball fans that I knew, such as Luddy McAllister and Shorty, followed the Dodgers, the team that had broken the color barrier by hiring Jackie Robinson and whose roster contained such notable black athletes as Roy Campanella and Big Don Newcomb. To Wade's blacks in the mid-fifties, the Dodgers, more than any other national organization or institution, represented the goals of equality and acceptance. By supporting the Yankees, Jerome courted the charge of racial apostasy.

Jerome was not merely a Yankee fan; he truly loved the game. Baseball was a vital part of his life. He had played sandlot ball as a young man, often against white teams or teams with white players, and he enjoyed recalling the excitement of his playing days. He followed the big league teams assiduously, reading the box scores of all the games of the previous day. He knew the personnel of most teams—the players, managers, and coaches—and could rattle off performance statistics of leading hitters and pitchers in both leagues. He remembered great plays, delighted in talking strategy, and believed the World Series was the most important event of the year, superseded only by a presidential election. To Jerome the major tragedy of the Second World War was the interruption of the careers of so many fine ballplayers.

I liked Jerome. He had a good sense of humor and told a good tale, and as one of the few Yankee fans in Wade, he was a kindred spirit. Wade's whites seldom supported the Yankees, partly because of their predictable success and partly, I suspect, because of the team name. I thought the Yankees were phenomenal. Already enamored with success, I admired their tradition, their depth, their combination of power hitting and superior pitching. Jerome and I spent hours talking about the Yankees—the power and speed of Mickey Mantle, the clutch hitting of Yogi Berra, the crafty moundsmanship of Eddie Lopat and Whitey Ford, the infield heroics of Phil Rizzuto and Bobby Richardson. We reveled in the Yankees' bench strength. We divided the club's roster to create "A" and "B" teams, each of which we thought capable of winning the pennant, or imagined a match between the Yankees and the National League All Stars.

During the years we talked, it never occurred to me that Jerome's allegiance to the Yankees carried a psychic cost—that he hoped to see a black in the Yankee lineup precisely because the team was, and for decades had been, baseball's best. When I did realize this, I also understood that I enjoyed talking with Jerome about the Yankees in part *because* the Yankees had no black players. I wasn't uncomfortable talking baseball with other blacks, although I knew that for them a Robinson, Banks, Mays, or Campanella was special. I understood that they admired these players not just as athletes, but as black athletes. It was impossible to talk with someone like Luddy, or with other black Dodger or Giant fans, and not sense their racial pride, although this dimension was rarely explicitly referred to.

From my perspective, race was absent from my discussions with Jerome, although I was a white youngster talking to a black man about an all-white Yankee team. Like most blacks of that era, Jerome carefully avoided remarks about racial relations at which whites might take affront. Our conversations had stretched over several seasons, and never once had Jerome expressed the desire to see an integrated Yankee team. Yet when in 1955 I read that the Yankees had broken their color line by signing the versatile outfielder-catcher Elston Howard, I knew the racial issue would be present in future talks with Jerome.

Since the press had allowed no one with the slightest interest in the game to escape the significance of Howard's signing and there was no avoiding the issue, the next time I saw Jerome I asked him what he felt about the newest Yankee. He fielded my question deftly, reciting Howard's statistics and telling me more about his ability to help the club than I really cared to know. Despite its length, it was a measured, serious response. Gone was the light-hearted, almost joking tone I had learned to expect from Jerome. I'll never forget the way he summed up his evaluation of Howard.

"They got a good man," he concluded. "I just wish they'd have done it sooner."

Jerome's mild criticism of the Yankees surprised me, for it was out of character for him to speak directly about the racial issue. I realized that Jerome was not just endorsing Howard as a black worthy of wearing the Yankee pinstripes. He was expressing disappointment that the Yankees had not hired a black earlier, that he had been forced to choose between loyalty to a team he had long supported and support of teams with less racist personnel policies. Our conversation about the Yankees' acquisition of Howard ended on that note. Jerome had voiced his previously unspoken disappointment and I understood him, even found myself in agreement. And for the first time I began to understand the price that he had paid to remain a Yankee fan.

Jerome and I continued to follow the Yankees together until I left for college. He never again referred directly to the team's racial policies, and neither did I. Yet his one comment had enlarged my racial perspectives much more than the ballpark heroics of a Mays or a Newcomb. Ballplayers were removed from my life—they were images on a television screen, names in the sports headlines. Jerome was a part of my world, someone I cared about and respected. Previously I had seen Jerome as a part of Granddaddy's world, a personification of the southern myth that members of both races preferred segregation. I began to comprehend that his remark about Elston Howard had much larger implications. It was Jerome's way of endorsing the school desegregation case that Daddy's and Granddaddy's friends spent so much time and energy condemning; it was his method of approving of the early stirrings of the civil rights movement. Jerome, the good black, the black Yankee fan, the older black I felt comfortable with under the old segregationist rules, was telling me that changes were coming, and that he believed them long overdue. Though it took some time to admit it, I gradually came to see that he was right on both counts.

For years after leaving Wade, I followed the Yankees and Elston Howard. He was the last star of the great Yankee teams of the late fifties and early sixties to retire. He spent the final years of his career playing with men of another generation, far less talented and charismatic than his old teammates. He saw the once proud Yankees eclipsed by even the lowly Mets. On reading of his death in 1980 I remembered Jerome and how he, Ellie Howard, and the Yankees had helped to ensure that mine would be the last generation of the segregated South.

My friendship with Jerome was always relaxed and enjoyable. We never talked about topics my family or the society considered serious. While I couldn't dismiss the feelings or opinions of Jerome, the fellow Yankee fan, I didn't have to worry about taking them seriously. Such, however, was not the case with Jerry and "Miss Carrie" McLean.

The McLeans lived a few hundred yards behind Granddaddy's store in a home that Jerry had, for the most part, constructed himself. To me Jerry and Carrie were Wade's most interesting couple. They were old; Miss Carrie seemed almost ancient. When I left Wade both were in their mid-seventies. I never called them Aunt or Uncle, titles paternalistic white southerners bestowed upon elderly blacks. Jerry and Carrie were, in the opinion of the family, above that.

Carrie McLean was the only black woman I ever heard whites address as Miss, the universal term of respect for all mature white women, married or single. It seemed natural to call her Miss Carrie. A retired schoolteacher, she had spent the better part of her life in the dilapidated frame schools of eastern North Carolina, struggling to educate her black pupils against the handicaps of an underfunded segregated school system. She long had been retired when I met her. Still, Miss Carrie looked and acted every inch the "school marm." Short, ramrod straight, she remained agile and quick. A strong, square face gave her a well-deserved look of determination. Her eyes, undimmed by age, peered from behind a pair of rimless spectacles. Her gray hair was pulled back in a bun. She wore inexpensive print dresses, neatly starched and ironed, over which always appeared a clean white apron. Her diction matched her crisp appearance, and her grammar, though not perfect, was superior to that of most of Wade's whites.

Miss Carrie ordered me about as if I were a student, her voice filled with humor and kindness but sharp enough to command my full attention. She never called me boy. To have done so would have

been a breach of propriety, in which Miss Carrie was a staunch
believer. Instead she called me Milton, a slight corruption of
Melton, my mother's maiden name, which, in typical southern fashion, had been given to me.

Miss Carrie would march into the store (she never merely walked
anywhere) and spot me leaned back against the wall in a ladder-
backed chair, reading a book or an installment of a Horatio Horn-
blower saga in Granddaddy's latest issue of the *Saturday Evening
Post.*

"Milton," she would order, "put that book down and get over
here. I do declare, you've always got your nose in a book."

Her tone would leave no doubt that she expected immediate service, while also indicating that she heartily approved of keeping
one's nose in a book whenever possible. Having obtained my attention, Miss Carrie would instruct me to fetch coffee, bread, or milk,
continuously critiquing my performance as I rushed to do her
bidding.

"Hurry up, Milton. I got to cook supper. I do declare, you're
slower than cold molasses."

Miss Carrie expected not only quick service, but exact attention.
When ordering meats she would indicate precisely which slice of
beef or pork she preferred. "Give me that slice at the back of the
tray, Milton. No, not that one. It doesn't look fresh. Pay attention
to what I'm telling you, son." I bobbed and weaved behind the meat
counter, trying to select Miss Carrie's choice.

She frequently interspersed her instructions with questions and
observations about my progress at school and plans for the future.

"You doing your best at school, are you, Milton? Always do your
best. You got some ability, son, don't you waste it playing around.
You get yourself all the education you can get. There's no such
thing as too much education, Milton. Just don't you read too much.
There's more to school than reading, you know."

Miss Carrie loved her education lecture, which I'm sure she had
delivered hundreds of times to promising pupils. I heard it dozens
of times, always delivered with equal fervor and conviction. I would

nod my agreement, or interrupt with an occasional "Yes, ma'am," in part because she echoed my family's sentiments and in part because disagreeing with Miss Carrie would have been unthinkable.

Jerry seemed much less formidable than Miss Carrie, perhaps because the entire community knew his life's story. Jerry was the child of a mulatto, and had been reared by one of the region's more prosperous white families. I was never told whether his foster parent was his natural father. If so, Jerry, like many blacks, was brought up in his white father's house, a home from which he was ejected when, as an adolescent, he was discovered playing in a bedroom with the farmer's young daughter.

As a young man Jerry worked as a tenant, married, and brought up a family. After the death of his first wife he met and wed Miss Carrie. His children had long since departed to points north and the promise of a better life, so he used his life's savings to build the small home in which he and Miss Carrie lived. Carrie's social security and teacher's retirement benefits, combined with the few dollars Jerry picked up at odd jobs, gave the couple some financial security.

Physically and emotionally, Jerry was Miss Carrie's opposite. He was a large man, over six feet, whose light yellow skin and green eyes revealed his parentage. Jerry seemed never to be serious. He laughed his way through life—teasing, joking, sharing a drink and sometimes a drunk, gabbing and gossiping, swapping stories with whites and blacks. Miss Carrie regarded work as a duty, while Jerry approached it as an unhappy inevitability. Miss Carrie set about her tasks with stoic acceptance, while Jerry tried to eliminate the drudgery from unavoidable labor. Their personality differences help explain why many whites called her Miss Carrie while her husband remained plain Jerry. Of course whites feared black males more and were reluctant to bestow any title upon them. Not once as a youth did I hear a white person of any age call a black man "mister."

Jerry was one of those blacks who frequently worked for my family. My earliest memories of him are of his plowing our garden, which he did several times a year. Jerry supervised my first and only experience with a mule-drawn plow, an opportunity for which I begged. For me it was great fun; for Jerry plowing represented a link to the past and a source of income. I struggled to keep the plow beneath the earth's surface while Jerry followed, laughing and shouting instructions to the poor bewildered mule. I remember hauling freshly raked pine straw in Jerry's black Chevrolet pickup truck, transporting aged appliances to the town dump, and making trips to Fayetteville to bring back purchases Granddaddy had made for the store. I remember Jerry at our house early in the winter morning on the annual hog-killing day, with his rifle in hand, setting out to slaughter animals whose carcasses would be denuded in vats of scalding water he had prepared in the predawn cold.

My relationship with Jerry was similar to the one I had with Jerome, but closer, more personal. Jerry was no sports fan, but he loved to talk—about the old days, village people, the weather, dogs, and hunting, all the common topics of casual conversation. His marvelously positive sense of humor revealed his natural optimism, and I enjoyed talking with him. While Jerry never ordered me about as Miss Carrie did, I knew that I was expected to do as he asked. I also knew that if I refused to follow his directions or showed him the slightest disrespect, and my father or grandfather learned of my behavior, I was in for trouble. Yet respect for Jerry, not fear of punishment, caused me to consider him something more than just another black man.

Like Miss Carrie, Jerry exercised the right to comment on my personal life and plans for the future. Jerry, however, never lectured me on the value of education. His approach was at once more casual and more direct. If he was in the store and I was slow to put down a book to wait on him or some other customer, Jerry was quick to admonish me.

"Your granddaddy's right. You're the slowest, laziest boy I know. You shore better keep reading them books so you can get a job where you don't have to work. Otherwise, you gonna starve to death."

I would respond in the same vein, pleading guilty of aversion to hard labor and assuring Jerry that as an adult I intended to avoid it if at all possible.

"Well," he would reply, "least ways you're honest about it," and if in the right mood, he would endorse my intentions concerning work with stories of his past labors.

Jerry never hesitated to instruct me in what he considered proper behavior, for he, like Miss Carrie, set great store upon propriety, although more so for others than for himself. He was more inclined to offer advice on some subjects than either my father or my grandfather. Like Granddaddy, Jerry appreciated good bourbon and occasionally overindulged. As a result, his warnings about the vices of alcohol were qualified by an appreciation of its merits.

"Liquor ain't no good for an old man like me," he would say, implying that a younger man might find it more enjoyable, if used in moderation. "It goes down easy, but you got to watch it, son. That stuff will sneak up on you, make you mean."

Jerry was less ambivalent about sex. His advice was simple. "You best keep that thing in your pants, boy, or you're likely to get into a heap of trouble."

He subscribed to the "two types of women" theory and warned me against "low-class white girls," whom he saw as a threat to my future. Once, upon learning that I had taken out a young lady of less than spotless reputation, he told me flatly, "You best leave that girl alone, boy, if you know what's good for you. She ain't nothing but trouble. First thing you know you'll have her knocked up and there'll be the devil to pay."

Jerry's attitudes about sex, or at least about my sex life, I quickly perceived, were no different from those of the adults in my family and the elders of the Presbyterian church. Unlike them, however, he had no trouble expressing his opinions in terms easily grasped. He was, in fact, my instructor in the folk culture. Unburdened by parental authority and the inhibitions of middle-class southern whites, he would cut to the heart of the issue with the bluntest language, and he expected his advice to be followed.

While I knew Jerry and Miss Carrie better than any other blacks in Wade I nevertheless knew them only on my terms. I saw them, like Jerome and Dora Lou, or any of Wade's black residents, outside their homes—at the store, in the community, or working at my house or at Ma Ma's. Black homes remained private, beyond the reach of white society—they formed a world of which I knew little. When delivering groceries to black families I was never asked to carry packages into their homes.

"Just you set the bags on the porch, son. My boy'll get 'em," I was told, or, "I can handle it from here. Don't you mind."

If I persisted with offers of help, I was politely but firmly refused.

"It's okay, really. We can manage."

Since I didn't enter black homes, I assumed that they were somewhat like mine and those of my friends. I knew that some poor blacks probably didn't have the furnishings that we did, that their houses were smaller, but if I thought about it at all, I thought that their homes were simply scaled-down versions of my own. Certainly I assumed that to be true of the homes of blacks like Jerry and Miss Carrie—people whom many whites respected, people with the same values as my family, people who lived in one of the neater black homes in the village.

Not until I was seventeen did Jerry and Miss Carrie invite me into their house. I will never forget that visit or the impact it had upon me. It was late November, near Thanksgiving. The weather had turned cold, dreary. I had delivered two bags of hog feed to Jerry, for he kept a pig or two in a pen near the woods that grew up to the edge of his back yard. Jerry came outside to watch me hoist the hundred-pound bag over my shoulder and led me to a small shed where he kept his feed. I flipped the sack from my shoulder and returned to the car for the second, and Jerry followed, chattering away. As I placed the second sack in the shed, Miss Carrie called from her back porch.

"Come on in here, Milton, have a piece of my pumpkin pie. It's still hot, just took it out of the oven."

Miss Carrie had a reputation as a fine cook. I had eaten her desserts before and knew the reputation was merited. But I had eaten them at my house, not hers. I felt a bit uneasy, but I wanted the pie, and besides, I knew that there was no way I could graciously decline her offer.

"Yes, ma'am," I replied and followed Jerry through the back porch and into the kitchen. The emotional impact of Miss Carrie's kitchen produced the physical responses one feels as a roller coaster begins its earthward plunge: the tightening of the stomach; the quick gasp for breath; the queazy, sinking feeling inside. Stunned by the appearance of the room, I searched for words while bursts of understanding exploded through my brain. Now I knew at least one of the reasons why blacks rarely asked whites into their homes. And just as quickly I understood the special significance of this invitation, which came just before I was to leave Wade, and while I was yet a juvenile, someone who could be taught and, perhaps, influenced by what he learned.

Nothing about my relationship with Jerry and Miss Carrie had prepared me for this moment. Nor had the exterior of their house, which I had seen so often; it was a small cottage, one of the nicer black residences in Wade. Miss Carrie had surrounded it with azaleas, nandenas, four o'clocks, and hydrangeas. In the front yard were beds of fall flowers, highlighted by a row of cockscomb, whose brilliant dried red plumes remain a vivid part of my memory of that day.

Despite the cold outside, the kitchen felt like an oven. Heat radiated from Miss Carrie's wood-burning cast iron stove, in which she had baked the pumpkin pie she offered. The room reeked of the odor of burning pine, and split pine logs were stacked neatly against one wall, ready to be fed into the stove, which also functioned as the heater in what was obviously the major living area in the house. The stove and the tin pipes stretching up from it to carry the smoke to the chimney filled a quarter of the room. Opposite the stove was a wooden table covered with a red and white checkered oilcloth, around which sat four worn cane-bottomed chairs. A hand pump and sink occupied another wall, a small refrigerator, the room's only other furnishing, stood near the sink.

Old newsprint covered sections of the wood-planked kitchen walls. I had never seen newsprint put to such use, and never would again except in Walker Evans's photographs of the home of Depression-era tenants. A newspaper portrait of Franklin Delano Roosevelt in a cheap dime store frame hung on one wall. Across from it in an old-fashioned wooden frame hung the picture of a fashionably dressed black woman of about fifty, whom I took to be Miss Carrie's mother. On another wall the glittering letters of a cardboard placard spelled out GOD BLESS OUR HOME. Beside it hung a color portrait of Jesus, his left hand raised, his right hand resting on his chest beneath a bleeding heart.

Appalled by what I saw, by the realization that these people whom I admired had so little, I wanted to somehow disappear from the scene, to sink through a crack in the floor and avoid this confrontation with reality. I felt as if I had invaded their privacy and discovered some long-kept secret, which I had. Miss Carrie sensed my hesitation, my ill-concealed uneasiness.

"Sit down, Milton, I'll slice the pie. You want some milk with it?"

"Yes ma'am, that would be fine," I replied, moving to the table with Jerry. Over my initial shock, I sat down to await my pie.

"Don't mind us, we've already had some," Miss Carrie said, placing an enormous slice of pie in front of me. "Now, tell me what you think, how does it taste?"

The pie was delicious, sweet and smooth-textured. "It's mighty good, Miss Carrie."

She smiled, pleased with my appreciation of her abilities as a cook of fine desserts. I began to relax a bit, and Miss Carrie took the opportunity to question me about her favorite topic.

"How are your grades, Milton? You keeping up with your school work?"

"Yes, ma'am," I responded between forkfuls of pie.

"You decided where you going to college yet?"

I could see Jerry was amused at my efforts to eat and talk with Miss Carrie, but he remained silent, unwilling to help me concentrate on the dessert by interrupting her inquisition.

"Yes, ma'am," I answered. "Probably East Carolina College."

"East Carolina?" she asked, a hint of disappointment in her voice. "Why not the university, Milton?"

"East Carolina has a good Air Force ROTC program, Miss Carrie," I explained. "I have to go in the service anyway, might as well go in an officer. I can retire in twenty years, then maybe teach."

I could tell I had made the correct response, that she saw my choice as logical and liked the idea of my teaching someday. By now I had finished the pie and was beginning to feel somewhat uncomfortable again, out of my element, as if the act of breaking bread together had given me a dispensation which had been used up. I wanted to return to my world, my white world of plenty and authority in which I felt comfortable.

"I've got to get back to the store now, Miss Carrie."

She ignored my remark. "Oh, have some more pie. We've got plenty. Besides, there's nobody here to eat it but Jerry and myself."

"No, ma'am," I insisted. "Really, I can't. The pie sure was good, but Granddaddy expects me back," I lied, seeking a gracious exit line.

"Very well, Milton, if you are sure you have to go," Carrie said, rising from the table.

Jerry and I followed her from the kitchen and through the back porch. Walking to the car, I called back, "Thanks again for the pie." I closed the car door and backed out of their yard.

After the visit Miss Carrie continued to monitor my academic progress while Jerry remained more concerned with my social activities. My relationship with them remained unchanged, but the visit in their home had confirmed my growing suspicions that I could not become a part of what had been, that I could never comfortably accept the racial etiquette that had been an essential reality in the world of my father and grandfather. It thus made inevitable my final rejection of the segregated South.

Not quite a year after my visit with Jerry and Miss Carrie I left for college, as planned. On my first two weekends back home I didn't see either Jerry or Miss Carrie, since I avoided spending much time at work. My first extended period home came with the Christmas holidays. As I had expected, I worked almost every day at the store, helping with the last rush of holiday shopping. Late one afternoon Jerry's pickup rolled up to the gas pumps and I went out to wait on him.

"Hello, Jerry," I called, glad to see him again. He had already alighted from the truck and begun to draw his gasoline himself. "I'll check your oil while you finish with the gas."

"That's all right," Jerry replied, not missing a beat and continuing to look at the nozzle stuffed into his truck's gas tank as if he expected it to overflow any second. "You go on back inside. I'll check the oil, Mr. Milton."

The word *mister* hammered me like a blow to the solar plexus. I had known Jerry for most of my eighteen years, and never once had he called me mister. I was always "boy," or occasionally Miss Carrie's more formal "Milton." During that time I had never heard Jerry address Daddy, whom he had watched grow to manhood, or Granddaddy, two years his junior, as anything other than mister. Jerry, I knew, was recognizing my position as an adult in the segregated South in the manner to which he was accustomed.

Immediately I realized that I could not accept the title, that I would never be a mister, at least not the mister that Jerry's use of the term implied. It wasn't that I felt too young to be so addressed by an older man, though that was a factor. I knew the real meaning of the term and understood clearly that if I accepted its use, even acquiesced in it, I would also be accepting the racial views of Daddy and Granddaddy, endorsing the inequities of segregation that produced the emotional turmoil I felt at the moment. Jerry was saying to me not "Now you are a man" but "Now you are a white man."

Searching frantically for an acceptable way to refuse the offered title, I laughed. "Going to college don't make me a *mister*, Jerry. I wish you wouldn't call me that."

For a moment we stood looking at one another across gaps of time and race, Jerry holding the gasoline nozzle, me with my hand on the hood of his truck. I knew that he knew what I meant. We were both, in our own way, the last generation. Mine was the last generation to come of age in the segregated South, his the last to have grown old in it. Both of us realized that change was inevitable, but for the moment the past offered the only safe retreat.

Jerry slowly replaced the nozzle in the gas pump and screwed the top onto the truck's gas tank, then turned to me. "Okay, boy. I got to run to town for your granddaddy. I'll see you later."

I did see Jerry later, perhaps four or five times, no more. I never really returned to live in Wade, not even for the summers. Within a few years of my departure from the village the change in racial relations that I knew eventually must come was in full swing. Removed from the village, no longer in personal contact with its people, I could judge the impact of the civil rights revolution only from what I saw and heard during brief visits home. Such visits were usually for a week or less, about every two years. Even then much of what I learned came from family members, as with each passing year my visits home became increasingly limited to that unit. Still, I could determine the basic patterns of change within the village, if not the impact of change upon individual lives.

Change was most obvious at the institutional level. The Civil Rights Act of 1964 immediately altered racial patterns and provided Wade's blacks with unprecedented economic opportunities and social freedom, though both were more freely exercised in Fayetteville and its suburbs than in the village of Wade. The Voting Rights Act of 1965 propelled blacks into the community's politics, and by the end of the decade blacks held major offices in a reorganized town government. Less than a decade after I left for college, Wade's schools were integrated, not without vociferous dissent from whites, but without violence. Freed from the restraints of legal segregation, with each passing year Wade's blacks asserted their new independence in an ever-increasing number of occurrences in village life. Gradually black participation in many community activities and events attained a level that would have been unimaginable for Jerry's generation.

At the level of personal interactions, however, change came

more slowly, and for some, not at all. For the young, the generation of blacks and whites who grew to maturity after the demise of legal segregation, integrated schools and public facilities did not necessarily result in more liberal racial attitudes. Yet slowly, haltingly, they began to reevaluate the relationship between the races and to move toward a different set of accommodations, one that accepted the opening to blacks of economic and educational opportunities previously closed. Socially, however, the old racial restrictions continued to be honored, even in many institutions, especially the church. Yet racial etiquette seemed somehow less important to many of the new generation. It endured, was observed, but no longer merited the constant justification and spirited defense an older generation had considered a sacred duty.

Members of the older generation, burdened with a segregated past, sought to accommodate themselves to the new reality, and to the future, as best they could. Whites continued to cling to their racial prejudices, some all the more tenaciously because of the drastic changes in a system which they so thoroughly understood, and in which they were so privileged. Some blacks, too, found change difficult, if welcome. Many, without position, wealth, or education, saw little change in the basic patterns of their daily lives. For them, the change had come too late. Meaningful change awaited their children, perhaps, and their grandchildren but had eluded them.

Yet there was no question that real change had occurred. The rigidly segregated society in which I had come of age had slipped quickly into the past. Practically overnight, certainly from the perspective of southern whites who clung to a revered past, the Wade I knew had become a place and period to be explored in the relative objectivity of seminars and dissertations on the history of race relations in the American South. Now geographically if not emotionally removed from village life, I welcomed the demise of the Wade of my youth. And I incorporated its passing into the unending process of assessing the psychological cost of growing up white in the segregated South, a process begun years earlier in the Wade that no longer existed.

Epilogue

I t was the winter of 1984, and we had returned home for Christmas Eve, my brothers and sisters and I, with our families. This
family reunion was an annual event, a night of feasting and gift
giving, of sharing childhood memories and parental hopes, of acknowledging the linkage of generations of family. The family was
my only remaining link with Wade, and it had changed. Granddaddy
died years ago in an automobile accident. It was a providential
death, actually, since no one else was injured. He had fallen and
broken a hip three years earlier, and had never recovered. Unable
to continue maintaining two businesses, Daddy had been forced
to sell the store. Ma Ma died within two years of Granddaddy's
death, as if she had suddenly tired of living. Of their generation, only
Olivia remained, now confined by deteriorating health to a nursing
home. A new generation, my daughters and nieces and nephews,
some of them already grown, gathered now to celebrate the
holidays.

The house, too, had changed. It had been completely re-
modeled, its exterior wrapped in brick veneer, its floors covered
with carpet, the kitchen, dining, and living areas enlarged, a new
tiled porch built across the front. The resulting structure barely
resembled the home of my youth. Inside, a large fireplace, outfitted
with an electric blower, filled the den with the warmth of a log fire,
the flames flickering silently behind glass doors.

The family milled about the den and kitchen, parents occasionally
warning over-eager children not to enter the living room and dis-

turb the gifts piled high beneath Mother's carefully decorated tree. The tree was positioned in the customary spot, squarely before the large windows so it could be seen from the road that ran in front of the house. Well into the afternoon, a brother opened a bottle of imported wine and poured a glass for all those who responded to his invitation to sample his latest find. With the help of daughters, granddaughters, and daughters-in-law, Mother set out the hors d'oeuvres: shrimp skewered by toothpicks stuck into a styrofoam cone covered with green paper foil, a variety of cheese balls, and a selection of meat salads, all with red and green garnishes. It was a signal that the festivities had officially begun.

As I stood in the kitchen my father approached me, pulling on a heavy nylon jacket. I recognized his restlessness, his unwillingness to be confined to the house while daylight remained. It was at night that he was a homebody. For him the opening of gifts was the highlight of the celebration, and it was far too early for that. Mother had decreed that gifts could be opened only after dinner, which would be preceded by hours of leisurely munching and sipping, of talking and laughing, of remembering.

"You want to go with me?" he asked, heading toward the kitchen door.

"Where are you going?" I responded, already reaching for my jacket, knowing that I would go, whatever his answer.

"Thought I'd drive down to Dora Lou's," he said, out the door now, stepping into a cold east wind, his hands jammed into his pockets. He moved quickly for a man of sixty-five who carried an extra thirty pounds or so, most of it about his middle.

"Got some lard out here I want to take her. Been here since Earl killed hogs."

Ah, yes, I thought. Hog killing time. The past lingers on. Earl was a farmer, an old friend of the family. The coming of winter required that he "kill hogs" for Daddy. It was a rural ritual Daddy enjoyed, and one he was determined not to let go, although it would have been far easier to buy his pork at a Fayetteville supermarket.

"We killed two hogs, about three weeks ago," he continued,

apprising me, the urban resident, of the continuing rural tradition. That, too, I suddenly realized, had become a ritual.

"Got this lard out here in the garage," he repeated himself. "I don't need it. Thelma never uses it any more, got to watch my cholesterol level. No use in it just sitting here and going rancid, though. Dora Lou can use it, she'll be glad to get it."

As he talked he walked into the open garage, past Mother's new Buick, through a door that opened into a large storage area adjacent to the garage. Inside were gardening tools, a refrigerator, fishing gear, and a variety of items I considered junk.

"You want a drink of bourbon?" he asked.

No French wines here, I thought, only drinks from the past. Good bourbon in a paper cup. No ice. The bottles were cold.

"No, thanks," I replied. "I don't drink much hard liquor any more."

He responded with a grunt and poured himself a shot.

"Here," he commanded, for I was still his son. "Help me lift this stand."

I moved forward and lifted the left side of the lard tin. He lifted the other handle with his free hand.

"Let's carry it to the truck."

Together we walked to his pickup truck, the lard tin swinging between us.

"Set it down," he ordered as we reached the rear of the vehicle, a huge new Chevrolet, blue and silver, with a blue camper shell on the truck bed. He opened the tail gate and we lifted the lard stand into the truck. I slammed shut the tail gate. We walked to the cab and climbed inside.

The truck's plush interior, color coordinated with the exterior, was complemented by the gadgetry—AM-FM radio, power windows, power locks, quartz clock, cruise control.

"Had to spend some money, huh?" I joked. "What do you need with two cars and a truck?"

"I got a deal," he said. "Besides, it comes in handy."

"For what?" I asked.

"Hauling things."

I let it drop. We drove up the road to Highway 301, turned right, passed the old elementary school for whites.

"The school's a dress factory now," Daddy said. "Some Yankee bought it. Works a lot of people in Wade when it's running, though."

We drove up the highway, past stores closed after Interstate 95, a mile to the east, made the highway obsolete and the sale of Granddaddy's store inevitable. We turned left onto a narrow street into the Bottom and rode past several houses. Each appeared to me unchanged in the twenty-five years since I left Wade.

"Hear the government's gonna fix up these houses in the Bottom," Daddy said. "Put in insulation, running water, bathrooms. Some of the people are against it, don't want their taxes spent on fixing up houses for blacks. Me, I think it's a damned good idea."

This last comment, I knew, was intended for my benefit.

He drove into the yard of a shotgun house and blew the horn. Two huge dogs were up and barking, straining at the chains that held them. Their chains were tied to poles between which were stacked pine slabs from Wade's lumber mill, which was no longer, Daddy told me, in the Tart family, but under corporate management.

"I hear some black woman from up North bought most of these houses in the Bottom," Daddy explained. "Bought them when the Tarts got out of the lumber business. Owned them about three or four years now."

The figure of an old woman, only slightly stooped, emerged from the front door. She wore a shirt and baggy blue pants. She walked down the steps and moved haltingly, with a rolling gait, toward the truck. Daddy opened his door and stepped out. I did the same. The dogs were in a frenzy, snarling and barking, leaping at us only to be hurled back by their chains. I stayed close to the door of the truck.

"Shut up, go lie down," the woman yelled at the dogs. She bent down, picked up a stick, and hurled it at them. Half obeying, they fell silent but continued to stand, straining at their chains.

"Mr. Merrian," the woman said in a voice I recognized as Dora Lou's. "Well I do declare."

Daddy had moved toward her, and I walked around the front of the truck to join them.

"How are you, Dora Lou," he returned her greeting. "Bet you don't know who this is," he said, nodding toward me.

"That Mr. Tim?" she asked.

"No, that's Melton, my oldest boy. You remember, the one who worked at my daddy's store."

"Is that Milton?" She moved a step closer. "Well, I do declare, it shore is. How you doing, Milton?"

"Just fine, Dora Lou," I said. "And you?"

"Oh, I'se old now, Milton. Ain't no fun being old, but I'm making it, I reckon. Where you living now, Milton?"

"I'm in Wilmington now."

"He's a professor at the university there," Daddy informed her, breaking into our conversation.

"That so?" Dora Lou indicated little interest in my profession. "I heared you be down to Alabama?" she asked, returning to the topic of my residence.

"I used to live in Mobile," I replied. "But we've been in Wilmington for some time now."

"You like it there, does you?"

"Yes, I do."

"You got chil'ren," she stated.

Mother or Daddy must have told her, I thought as she continued before I could respond.

"Girls, I believe. How old they now, Milton?"

"The oldest is eighteen; she graduated from high school last year. She's at the University of North Carolina now. My youngest is fourteen, in junior high."

"Well, I declare. You done got grown chil'ren, Milton. Don't seem like no time you was minding the store, nothing but a boy yoself. Yes sir, I 'member how Mr. Lonnie used to git on you 'bout being so slow."

She laughed, then turned abruptly toward the house and yelled.

"Jimbo, come on out here, Jimbo."

In a moment Jimbo walked from the house to join us, followed by a woman of roughly his age. He wore sneakers and a blue cotton work shirt and pants, the woman a simple print dress. She stood behind him, arms wrapped about her body to ward off the wind.

"Jimbo, you know who this is?" Dora Lou asked her son, pointing at me.

Jimbo leaned forward to get a better look.

"Yeah, I think I does. That's Milton, ain't it?" he said to me.

"Yes, Jimbo, it's me." I stepped forward to shake his hand. "How you doing?"

"Oh, pretty good, I guess."

"He be working over to Fayetteville," Dora Lou interjected. "That's his wife," she continued, gesturing toward the woman behind Jimbo. She gave no name.

"And Jenny?" I asked Dora Lou.

"Jenny stays with me, too. She be over to a friend's house. You 'member her boy Cooter?"

"Yes. He must be grown now."

"He most near forty," Dora Lou laughed. "He work over to Fayetteville. Live there, too."

"I thought those dogs were going to eat us up," I said, turning to Jimbo and desperately trying to break out of our ritualized conversation.

"Yeah. They mean dogs, all right," Jimbo replied. "We keeps them tied to the wood pile so's nobody don't steal our slabs."

Daddy interrupted my attempted conversation, much to my relief. "Got something for you, Dora Lou. Thought I'd bring it by for Christmas. Jimbo, help me get it out of the truck."

Daddy moved to the back of the truck and opened the tailgate. Jimbo followed him.

"Reach in there and slide that lard stand over," Daddy said, and Jimbo did. I moved up to the tailgate and helped Jimbo lift the stand to the ground.

"I shore does thank you, Mr. Merrian," Dora Lou said.

"I just thought you could use it." Daddy acknowledged her

thanks. "Well, we better get back. I've got the whole family home for Christmas, and Thelma'll be serving dinner soon."

I took my cue, walked back to the truck, and climbed in the cab. Daddy slipped under the wheel and cranked the motor, his door still open.

"You all have a good Christmas," he said, and began to back out of the yard.

Again, the dogs barked and lunged forward against their chains. Dora Lou and Jimbo waved goodbye, and the woman turned and walked toward the house. Jimbo stooped, grabbed a stick, and tossed it at the dogs. Daddy pointed the truck toward the highway, and we headed home. We rode several minutes without speaking, each aware that the other was thinking of the past. Daddy broke the silence.

"Well, I guess Dora Lou was happy to get that lard."

"Yes," I replied, "I guess she was."

There was nothing left for me to say that my father would understand. He was pleased with his gift, and from his perspective, I know, he had reason to be. He remained, spiritually, emotionally, a resident of the Wade I had left and to which I could never return. Yet it was in that Wade, that village past, that our present bond was forged, and it was in that Wade that the bond existed still. And so, aware of and linked by our separate pasts, we rode toward home and the celebration of a family Christmas.

Afterword

For the past twenty years I have lived and worked in Wilmington, North Carolina, a still-pleasant port city now simultaneously ensnared and enthralled by the material prosperity that often accompanies rapid growth. My family and I came to Wilmington in part because the Cape Fear River links it to Wade, and thus to my past. Wilmington, the state's largest port and until the early twentieth century its largest city, sits on the east bank of the Cape Fear River, approximately fifteen miles upriver from the Atlantic. An inland community some 110 miles upriver, Wade had its beginnings as a river landing just above the fall line, and the Cape Fear continued to link the two very different communities throughout my youth. Mama, my maternal grandmother, and my great-aunt Olivia had aunts who lived in Wilmington. As girls they visited their aunts in the summers, and Mama attended school for a year in Wilmington, staying with an aunt in a home that still stands on the corner of Sixth and Princess Streets. I distinctly remember soon after receiving my driver's license chauffeuring Mama and Olivia to Wilmington to visit relatives who resided in one of the homes beneath the live oaks of Market Street.

My father and mother loved Wilmington and, even more, the beaches that lie just east of the city. Almost every summer, we went as a family—Mama, Olivia, my father and mother, my siblings and I—to those beaches to spend a week in a rental cottage. Occasionally there were day trips to Wilmington and the beaches. After attending Sunday services at Wade's Bluff Presbyterian Church, my father would announce that for lunch (always called dinner) we would drive to Uncle Henry

Kirkum's Oyster Roast, a rustic seafood restaurant on the Intercoastal Waterway south of Wilmington. While infrequent, such adventures, which invariably included Mama and Olivia, were memorable. I now live in a home on the Intercoastal Waterway on what was once Kirkum property. A snapshot of me at twelve, posed with my siblings against a crude wooden frame used to dry the gill nets that supplied fish for Uncle Henry's kitchen, adorns the photo gallery in my mother's den and is tucked into the corner of the dresser mirror in my bedroom. Uncle Henry's, the last of the region's true oyster roasts and within easy walking distance when my family and I moved into our current home twelve years ago, burned to the ground a few years later to be replaced this year by the home of yet another family enticed to the region by the beauty of its waters and salt marshes.

The Wade of my youth and the Wilmington of my present are connected by more than the Cape Fear and fond memories. Both communities were shaped by the same powerful forces of history, especially by the racial conflict that is at the heart of the region's, and the nation's, past. This historical linkage between Wade and Wilmington is perhaps most apparent in a series of events in the last years of the nineteenth century, events that created the segregated Wade in which I came of age, and events that continue to impinge upon my personal and professional life as a historian and university administrator attempting to grapple with their meaning and significance in the past, for the present, and into the future.

Racial violence in Wilmington in 1898 was the catalyst for, if not the ultimate cause of, these events. In the approximate quarter century between the end of Reconstruction and the establishment of legal segregation in North Carolina, Wilmington remained the state's largest city, developing a large, politically active and economically vibrant black population. With the aid of black voters in Wilmington and elsewhere, in 1894 a "Fusion" coalition of Populists and Republicans seized control of the North Carolina legislature from the Democrats who represented the state's planter-industrial elite. Meeting the following year, the newly-elected Fusionist legislature liberalized registration laws, expanding the franchise for blacks and poor whites, thus enabling a Fusionist slate to wrest control of Wilmington's municipal government from the Democrats in the elections of 1896. In 1897, Wilmington had a truly biracial municipal government, with three black aldermen, two all-black fire companies, several black policemen and numerous other black civil servants. John Dancy, the black collector of customs appointed by President William McKinley, was the city's highest paid and one of its most influential public officials. Alex Manly published the state's only daily black newspaper, and a black middle class composed of educators, lawyers, clergymen, skilled craftsmen, merchants, and businessmen was an integral part of the city's economic and political institutions.

Given the racial views of white America, especially those of the white South, a reaction was inevitable, and it came with a vengeance in 1898. Determined to regain control of Wilmington and the state, the Democratic party launched a stridently racist campaign, portraying blacks as the rapacious destroyers of white civilization, as an insidious evil against which the whites of North Carolina could be protected only by Democratic leadership. Wilmington came to symbolize the statewide Democratic effort to regain political control. Using Alex Manly's editorial charge that black males accused of rape were often victims of white women who leveled the charge to avoid social ostracism upon the discovery of their liaison, Democratic orators whipped the emotions of Wilmington's white voters to a fever pitch.

Victory in the November 8 election did not appease Wilmington's Democratic forces, and on November 9, they presented black leaders with a "White Man's Declaration of Independence," which called for the immediate resignation of the municipal government and the acceptance of white supremacy. The following day the Federal government, despite pleas for intervention, stood by as a mob of whites led by some of Wilmington's most respected and influential citizens destroyed Manly's newspaper and burned the building in which it was housed, killed at least nine blacks and drove others from their homes, forcefully expelled from the city both black and white political and business leaders opposed to Conservative Democratic rule and white supremacy, and used paramilitary forces to remove from office Wilmington's duly elected city government.

The racial violence in Wilmington in November of 1898 was but the prelude for a statewide, race-based campaign to bring North Carolina into the ranks of the segregated South. Using the racial rhetoric and tactics of intimidation so successfully employed in Wilmington in 1898, the Democrats swept into power in 1900 and wielded that power to disenfranchise black voters and to segregate by law the state's black citizenry. A half century later, these laws, with various modifications, and the racism upon which they rested, governed the social, economic, and political behavior of the citizenry, black and white, of the Wade in which I spent my youth.

The years between my departure for college in 1959 and the present have treated Wade and Wilmington differently, but the two communities continue to struggle with the legacies of racism and segregation. Wilmington is in the midst of an economic and cultural renaissance, barely able to cope with the problems of growth. Populated by affluent locals and retirees from the North, gated communities of near-palatial homes line the Intercoastal Waterway and, increasingly, the eastern bank of the Cape Fear below the city. The downtown region has been reborn, with block after block of its antebellum and Victorian townhouses restored to their former grandeur, their residents joining tourists and a local professional workforce to support a proliferating number of eateries, bars, clubs, and specialty shops. Between the Waterway and the downtown area, suburban sprawl threatens to annihilate the remaining pine lands. A thriving movie industry has revitalized the region's arts community, proliferating theatrical groups compete for performance venues, clubs and bars are awash with local musicians, and art galleries blossom along downtown streets and in suburban malls.

The city's affluence, and that of tiny New Hanover County in which it is located, is not distributed equally. While the area has a growing black middle class, a predominately black population remains in public housing units and is largely unaffected by the economic development of the downtown area and the primarily white suburbs. The city's black population, over 50 percent in 1898, is today slightly more than 30 percent, and New Hanover County's black population, now only 20 percent, continues to decline as rising land prices inevitably force black landowners to sell to developers.

The approaching centennial anniversary of Wilmington's racial violence has forced both the black and white communities to face the city's heritage of racism and segregation as they prepare to commemorate the events of 1898. Ongoing debates over the nature of that commemoration have sparked passionate responses from both sides of Wilmington's continuing racial divide, debates in which I have participated as a historian, a university representative, and a citizen of Wilmington with vivid memories of a segregated Wade. Articulate young blacks call for reparations for the wrongs of the past while descendants of the city's 1898 white elite attempt to justify the actions of their forebears. Community and institutional leaders struggle to create a constructive stance for the institutions they represent. Even the wording used to describe the events of 1898, "race riot," "racial violence," "coup d'etat," "massacre," each a term with passionate connotations for some constituency, sparks heated debates. Academics have been denied the right to speak to certain groups because of their views about the events of a hundred years ago. Politically active whites have threatened to tear down any monument erected to honor those blacks killed in the rioting, although the state of North Carolina finally plans to erect a marker dedicated to Alex Manly and his paper as a part of scheduled commemorative ceremonies.

As a historian, I have struggled to convince those on both sides of the racial divide to view the past objectively, to use it and any commemorative undertakings as means to achieve a common goal of creating a less racially divided society. It is not an easy argument to sustain, for in Wilmington, as throughout the South, the differing perceptions of the past still segregate the community. It matters deeply to black and white Wilmingtonians how the events of 1898 are publicly portrayed, how they are approached in the city's churches, and how they are taught in its schools.

While Wade, too, faces the problems of a past of segregation and a present marked with continuing racial prejudice, it has fared far less well economically than Wilmington during the last four decades. Throughout my senior year in high school, two or three times a week I would rise early in the morning, go to my grandfather's store, and pump hundreds of gallons of gas into vehicles used by construction

crews building Interstate 95, which ran to the east of Wade, within
sight from our kitchen window. Once completed, the interstate deprived Wade of an economic reason for being. One by one, the stores
in the community closed as people took the interstate to nearby
Fayetteville to buy even the necessities of daily life. Also accessible
via the interstate, industries relocating from the North attracted
Wade's local work force, a process accelerated by the demise of legal
segregation in the sixties. Spurred by school desegregation, consoli-
dation, which cost the village its schools in the 1950s, continued to
move the schools attended by Wade's children even farther from the
community in the 1960s and '70s.

While the interstate destroyed Wade as an economic community, the
Cape Fear River prevented the town from being sucked into Fayetteville's
suburbs, a circumstance for which many of Wade's citizens, white and
black, are exceedingly grateful. Cumberland County is split in two by
the river, with Fayetteville and Fort Bragg on the west bank. Wade is
situated in the eastern, and still largely agricultural, section of the county,
twelve miles north of the nearest bridge. Fayetteville's growth has been
to the southwest and north along the west bank of the river, along the
eastern edges of the sprawling Fort Bragg military complex. Thus, while
Wade's residents primarily now earn their livelihood west of the river,
few newcomers attracted to the region by Fayetteville's economic prosperity have chosen to settle in Wade.

During the 1997 Christmas holidays I drove from Wilmington to
Wade and took what has become an almost annual pilgrimage through
the community with my father. I am especially aware of the passage
of time on this occasion, for my father, who is seventy-nine, has recently undergone major surgery that nearly cost him his life. The Wade
I see is like many of the faces that confront me when I attend my mother
and father's church: vaguely familiar, yet ultimately unrecognizable.
In the central section of the community, which remains white, the old
school house has long since been demolished, as have several of the
general stores. Many of the houses have been torn down, both prominent homes and framed cottages. My great-grandfather's Victorian
home has been removed and restored on a site miles from the village.

Tart's sawmill, first sold to a corporate owner, has finally closed, its now dilapidated commissary boarded up, its large metal garage now used to store hay. No new homes replace those that have been demolished in the heart of the old community, and a mobile home park sits off the street near my grandfather's old home. The heart of the white Wade I knew is now bleak and ugly. An exception is the Bluff Presbyterian Church, which, like its counterparts in the black community, Wesley Memorial Chapel and Mt. Olive Baptist Church, has been expanded and refurbished. The village's only remaining institutions, these churches are the social glue that holds the community together. Other improvements, financed primarily by federal funds, are evident. The old post office has been replaced by a more commodious brick structure. Some federally funded projects provide Wade's citizens services not available in the Wade of my youth. Wade now has a medical center, staffed with a nurse and a physician, and a well-equipped volunteer fire department. All of these institutions are located in the white section of the community.

The appearance of the black community, however, has improved. Its streets have been paved and marked; the tiny framed homes of the Bottom and across from my grandfather's store have been refurbished, supplied with indoor plumbing, and connected to the community's water system. Funds for the paving, the refurbishing, and for the water system came largely from federal grants. Now almost the size of Bluff Presbyterian, and with a new brick façade, Wesley Memorial is a more impressive structure than the white Baptist church. In the area between my father's home and my grandfather's store, the few black homes of my youth have been transformed into an entire community, which also boasts paved streets. My tour of the village leaves no doubt in which racial community the power and money of Wade continue to reside, but it also reveals substantial change.

It is not just the physical appearance of Wade that has changed. Reincorporated as a town more than two decades ago largely to be able to obtain federal funds, Wade now has a biracial town council, which is currently composed of a black man, two white women, and two white men. One of the white men is my father, who, missing poli-

tics after eight years on the county planning board and perhaps moti-
vated by the fact that my mother had previously served two terms on
the council, ran for a seat on the Wade town council in 1997. He was
elected without campaigning and while in the hospital recuperating
from surgery, collecting a grand total of eighty-eight votes. Huel
Aiken, a black former council member, was elected mayor, leading the
ticket with well over two hundred votes from a predominately white
electorate.

Such a political arrangement would have been unimaginable in the
Wade in which I came of age, as well as illegal. I remember Huel as
one of segregated Wade's teenagers, about three or four years older
than I, whom I saw frequently in my grandfather's store. Yet my father
seems perfectly at ease about serving under Huel on the council, and
with Kevin Herring, the black council member, a native of Wade a bit
younger than I. Ironically, my father's ready acceptance of political
integration stems in part from his essentially paternalistic racial views,
which have changed little, and which always allowed for cooperative
working relationships with blacks, especially those he knew well or
who were members of the community. In this respect, my father's racial views now differ from those of my mother. Life in an integrated
society has modified her racial views, and she frequently expresses a
more profound understanding of the corrosive effects of racism on
the human spirit.

Before returning to Wilmington, I visited with Allen Smith. Like
my father, though slightly younger, Allen has lived his entire life in
Wade, while earning his living in Fayetteville, an employee of the
Veteran's Hospital. He and his wife Vernelle raised their family of seven
children in Wade, and I remember well Sarah, their oldest, who is four
years younger than I. Sarah and the older children attended segregated
schools, as I did; her younger siblings, like mine, went to integrated
schools. Allen came from one of Wade's most respected black families,
respected by whites and by blacks, and his father is discussed in this
work. Most of Allen's siblings left Wade. He stayed, I suspect, for several reasons, not the least of which were Vernelle, a beautiful young
woman; federal employment that provided economic security beyond

that available to most Wade residents, black or white; and the emotional security of remaining close to his mother and father.

Allen and Vernelle now live within sight of my mother and father's house, in a neat, white-frame, ranch-style home. I have asked my father to call Allen to see if he would mind a visit, for Allen, medically retired for some time, suffers from a degenerative muscular disorder and has difficulty walking. Allen agrees, and on the day of my visit to Wade, Vernelle comes over to my mother and father's with two of her daughters and a grandchild. They have come for turnips from my father's garden. Exchanges of food between the Smith and McLaurin families, it seems, now occur with some regularity, and more so with Mary, Allen's sister, retired from a career as a cook in the D.C. area to her father's homeplace, who occasionally supplies my father a coconut cake or some other baked goods in return for some of his vegetables. The families are neighbors, in most of the ways that the word implies. Although I have spoken to Allen by phone that morning, I ask Vernelle if the noon meeting he suggested is fine with her, since Allen had expressed some concern that she might not be there. I have not seen Vernelle in almost forty years; she remains an imposing woman. She introduces me to two of her daughters and a grandchild. The daughters are much younger than I; the oldest is a Christmas visitor I vaguely remember. Vernelle asks if I can come later in the afternoon, when she can be there. I say, "Of course."

I call on Allen at four that afternoon, knocking at the door in the carport. After a moment, Allen opens the door, then turns his walker to shuffle back to his couch in the den.

"Come on in, McLaurin," he calls back to me. "I'm in the den watching TV." His speech is slightly slurred, but I understand him easily. I enter the house and step into the den; he motions for me to sit in an upholstered chair while he eases himself onto his couch.

"Let me cut this darn thing off," he says, reaching for the TV remote. "I'm just watching something till Vernelle gets back. Tell you the truth, there ain't much on to watch now days."

I quickly agree, and express my thanks for his willingness to speak with me.

"Allen," I continue, " I'm writing something about Wade, and I've asked to talk with some people. Actually, I'm writing something for a book about Wade I did some time ago."

I don't ask if he has read it, and he doesn't volunteer any information.

"Yeah," he says, "your daddy told me."

I glance around the comfortably furnished room, the place where Allen and Vernelle obviously spend much of their time. On the fireplace mantle is a row of portraits. I recognize Sarah in a formal portrait of her family. She appears to be a woman of about forty-five in the photograph.

"Are those all of your children?" I ask, nodding toward the portrait gallery.

"Yes," he says. "That's Sarah and her family over there," he adds, pointing to the portrait that had caught my eye.

"I remember Sarah," I say. "She was younger than me, but I remember her. I remember her brother, he was the next, I believe. I can't remember any more of the children, Allen."

"We had seven children. Four of them live in Charlotte now. One of the boys passed. The youngest girl lives in Fayetteville. You wouldn't have known her."

"I met her with Vernelle this morning," I reply.

"Allen, I rode through Wade with Daddy this morning," I continue, shifting the conversation to my concerns. "It seems to me there is little to do here anymore, that everybody works in Fayetteville or Dunn. All the stores are closed now, except for Granddaddy's, and it appears to be a convenience-type store now. Overall, it seems to me that the old white section of Wade is declining, but it looks like the black sections of town seem better off."

"Well," he responds, "you about got it right. There aren't no jobs in Wade anymore. And we do need a store. I don't go to your granddaddy's place any more. Their prices are too high, and I don't think they appreciate your business. So we shop in Fayetteville now, like most everybody else."

We reminisce a bit about his father, and he tells me he died in the early eighties, well into his nineties. We talk about my grandfather, and Allen recalls him telling him he could always buy whatever he wanted. "I appreciated that. Used to, folks would help you out. It's just different now."

"You know," he continues, "a man at work once asked me if I could lend him twenty-five dollars. I asked him if there wasn't someone in his community who could lend him the money. He said, no, there wasn't. I asked him how long he had lived in that community. He said about twenty years. I told him if he couldn't find somebody in that community that would lend him twenty-five dollars after living there twenty years, then he needed to move."

I decide to move the conversation from memories to race relations.

"Allen, a lot has changed in Wade since I left. I've been gone almost forty years. When I come to Wade now, I just visit with Mother and Daddy. I don't know the community any more, can't even recognize a lot of the people I knew as a boy. And of course, segregation's gone. But what about race, how big an issue is that now?"

He pauses just a moment before replying. "Oh, it's still there. It's always there, just below the surface, in just about everything."

"I understand Kevin Herring serves on the town council now, and Huel Aiken is the mayor. That's a big change. How do you think Wade's whites respond to this?"

"Well, Huel, he seems to be pretty well liked," he replies quickly, a hint of a smile in his voice.

Then, looking me directly in the eyes, he continues, his tone more thoughtful. "There are some who aren't happy with the situation, but they can't do nothing about it. For the most part, we get along. There's people of my race I don't want nothing to do with, just like there's people of your race that you don't want nothing to do with. And there's people of your race that I'd rather be with than some of my race. But the racism is still there."

He pauses a beat in his response, glancing away, as if searching for just the right words to capture the way in which race and racism continue to impact the community.

He faces me again and speaks slowly, forcefully, the words coming from deep within him. "It's in you, and it's in me, and that's the truth, down there inside us. That's just the way it is."

"Yes, Allen," I acknowledge, "that's the truth. It's a hard truth. But do you think things are better?"

"Oh, yeah, it's better. We can visit now, like we're doing. I can go to your daddy's now, and he can come here, and that's changed, and that's good. And there's other things changed, like now I lock myself in the house when Vernelle's gone, 'cause you don't never know what people will do nowadays, and I can't move like I used to."

He has provided me a graceful exit from the topic of race, and I take it. We talk for a few more minutes about the decline of small town family values, and then Vernelle arrives. She apologizes for arriving late and sits in a chair at the end of the couch, joining the conversation, which drifts back to their children. Vernelle counts off the grandchildren and great-grandchildren for me, with obvious pride. I ask if they see them much.

"Oh, yes," she laughs. "It seems like we stay on the road to Charlotte."

It is growing dark outside, and I rise to make my exit. "I've got to get back to Mother's," I say. "I'd like to leave so I can get home before it's very late."

Allen begins to struggle to his feet. I urge him not to do so, but he does anyway, grabbing the walker and moving toward me. We shake hands; his grip remains strong. As Vernelle opens the door for me, I thank them both for having me in their home.

"Don't let this be your last visit," Allen says, as I step into the doorway and turn to answer him. I know his request is layered with meaning.

"I'll try not to."

I get in the car, and am filled with a deep, sorrowful anger. It does not diminish as I drive from Wade to Wilmington to continue to struggle with the difficult necessity of confronting our separate pasts.